D1447936

THE WITNESS OF LUKE TO CHRIST

In Memory of

MY FATHER

1864-1946

THE WITNESS OF LUKE TO CHRIST

N. B. STONEHOUSE, TH.D.

Professor of New Testament in
Westminster Theological Seminary, Philadelphia

1953

WM. B. EERDMANS PUBLISHING COMPANY

GRAND RAPIDS, MICHIGAN

First Edition - April 1951

Second printing, April, 1953

This American edition published by
special arrangement with Inter-Varsity
Fellowship (Tyndale Press), London, England

PHOTOLITHOPRINTED BY CUSHING - MALLOY, INC.
ANN ARBOR, MICHIGAN, UNITED STATES OF AMERICA
1953

PREFACE

THIS volume contains, in considerably expanded form, the special lectures which the author had the honour of delivering under the auspices of the Free Church College in Edinburgh during the last week of April, 1949. The public lectures were largely confined to materials presented in Chapters II, III, IV, VI and VII. The opportunity of lecturing on and discussing 'The Gospel at Nazareth' (the substance of Chapter IV) in Sheffield University on 3 May 1949, at the invitation of the Department of Biblical Studies, is also gratefully recalled as having contributed to the final result. Previously I had spoken somewhat less formally on the general theme of the book at the Annual Summer Conference conducted by Hope College and Western Theological Seminary in Holland, Michigan, in August, 1947. It is a pleasure to give expression here to my gratitude for these invitations and my continued appreciation of the exceptional kindness shown me by members of the faculties of these institutions when I was their guest.

The studies themselves were initiated as far back as the year 1941 when I enjoyed a leave of absence from my regular duties at Westminster and undertook an investigation of the distinctive testimony of the canonical Gospels. The publication of *The Witness of Matthew and Mark to Christ* in 1944 was a direct result, and the present volume may be viewed as a sequel to the treatment of the first two Gospels.

The title of the book is intended to suggest that the basic concern has been exegesis of the sacred text and that therefore the chapters that follow are presented as studies in the interpretation of the Third Gospel. The importance of turning back again and again to the Bible itself to discover what it actually says can hardly be exaggerated. Contemporaneous study of the New Testament abounds with modernizations of Jesus and the Gospels which betray a tragic lack of exegetical fidelity. Conservatives may and ought to do better, because they generally approach the exegetical problems with a sympathy rooted in their commitment to the Christian presuppositions of the authors of

Scripture. But conservatives are prone to a traditionalism which is uncritical of the past and is not sufficiently alert to the distinction between what is written and what may have been erroneously inferred from the biblical text. In particular it has seemed to me that Christians who are assured as to the unity of the witness of the Gospels should take greater pains to do justice to the diversity of expression of that witness. It is a thrilling experience to observe this unity, to be overwhelmed at the contemplation of the *one* Christ proclaimed by the four evangelists. But that experience is far richer and more satisfying if one has been absorbed and captured by each portrait in turn and has conscientiously been concerned with the minutest differentiating details as well as with the total impact of the evangelical witness.

As occupied with Christ, and therefore with Christianity, this work deals with a profound and broad theme. Yet there are self-imposed limitations which I trust will be kept in view by the reader. The book is basically concerned with exegesis, as I have stressed, but it does not make the pretence of dealing with all the major exegetical problems which have emerged in the study of Luke. There is also present a subordinate apologetic interest. Exposition of the truth indeed can hardly fail to be a defence of it. But it is beyond the scope of this book to discuss the broad subject of Christian presuppositions or to set forth a comprehensive argument for the truth of biblical Christianity. My own goal has been the more modest one of dealing with the witness of Luke to Christ in the context of certain modern interpretations of Christ and the Gospel.

My hearty thanks are expressed to Professor John H. Skilton, my co-worker in the New Testament Department in Westminster, who graciously read the manuscript and gave me the benefit of his observations and to Miss Margaret S. Robinson who kindly assisted in the preparation of the typescript. I am also deeply grateful to my wife for encouragement and help from the initiation of the work to its completion.

N. B. S.

CONTENTS

ABBREVIATIONS

AV	Authorized Version
ARV	American Revised Version (1901)
BTS	Biblical and Theological Studies: Princeton
DB	Dictionary of the Bible (Hastings)
DCG	Dictionary of Christ and the Gospels (Hastings)
EQ	The Evangelical Quarterly
ERV	English Revised Version (1881)
ExGT	Expositor's Greek Testament
GThT	Gereformeerd Theologisch Tijdschrift
HB	Handbuch zum Neuen Testament (Lietzmann)
HC	Hand-Commentar zum Neuen Testament (Holtzmann)
ICC	International Critical Commentary
ISBE	International Standard Bible Encyclopedia
JBL	Journal of Biblical Literature
JThS	Journal of Theological Studies
KNT	Kommentaar op het Nieuwe Testament (Grosheide and Greijdanus)
KV	Korte Verklaring der Heilige Schrift
MM	Vocabulary of the Greek New Testament (Moulton and Milligan)
MNT	Moffatt New Testament Commentary
PThR	Princeton Theological Review
SBK	Kommentar zum Neuen Testament aus Talmud und Midrasch (Strack and Billerbeck)
SNT	Schriften des Neuen Testaments (J. Weiss)
TWNT	Theologisches Wörterbuch zum Neuen Testament (Kittel)
RSV	Revised Standard Version of the New Testament (1946)
WC	Westminster Commentaries (Lock)
WMMC	The Witness of Matthew and Mark to Christ
WThJ	Westminster Theological Journal
ZNW	Zeitschrift für die Neutestamentliche Wissenschaft

Biblical quotations are taken for the most part from the English Revised Version

THE WITNESS OF LUKE TO CHRIST

CHAPTER I

INTRODUCTION

THE witness of Luke to Christ has always possessed a high degree of fascination. Although its author intimates that he was not a member of the circle of disciples who were associates and confidants of Jesus in the days of his flesh, the work has won universal acclaim because of its distinctive message and its literary beauty and charm. While perhaps never attaining the popularity of Matthew, it has likewise by no means shared the relative obscurity of Mark.

Renan called the Gospel according to Luke 'the most beautiful book in the world.'[1] Certainly its literary qualities have been universally recognized as of a very high order. Harnack, who was occupied more fully than any other scholar in this century with the linguistic character of the Lucan writings, declares that Luke 'was a master of language'. And after observing how the author with masterful artistry 'accommodated his style in different portions of his work to the scene of action and the dignity of his subject matter,' he concludes that 'in respect of its style this work can be compared with the best literary productions of the Hellenico-Roman period.'[2] His skill as a narrator, moreover, is such as to charm every one, the humble reader as well as the specialist in linguistics and literature.

The fascination of this book is, however, more than that of a superficial beauty which tends to vanish as one lives with it and hears what it is concerned to say. Its contents also grip the reader. This is no doubt true because it tells so delightfully the incomparable story of Jesus the Christ. But it is also bound up with the consideration that Luke reports much that is not to be learned

[1] *Les Évangiles*, 1877, p. 283: 'C'est le plus beau livre qu'il y ait.'
[2] *The Acts of the Apostles*, 1909, pp. xxxvii f.

from the other records. It is not inconsequential in this connection to observe that Luke is the most voluminous contributor to the New Testament, the two parts of his great work constituting more than one-fourth of the volume. His Gospel is the longest book in the New Testament. In the Text of Nestle Mark takes only about fifty-seven pages, John about seventy, and Matthew eighty-seven, while Luke takes nearly ninety-five pages. The autograph of Luke, assuming that it was written on a papyrus roll, must have run to more than thirty feet, which apparently is longer than was ordinarily considered practicable.[1] It should not be rashly supposed that the length of Luke is due to a tendency towards verbosity. Actually Luke is far more concise than Mark at many points. The length of Luke was determined by his judgment as to the materials which he was required to present in order to accomplish his purpose.

The greater extent of Luke is accounted for partially by the distinctiveness of the birth and resurrection narratives which are more than twice as long as those in Matthew. But the most decisive factor is the singularness of his treatment of the public ministry of Jesus. While Luke devotes somewhat less space than Mark, and considerably less than Matthew, to the narration of the Galilean ministry and of the events which occurred in Jerusalem until the death of our Lord, it takes approximately three times as much space to set forth the story of the approach from the borders of Galilee to the arrival in Jerusalem. One must look, accordingly, especially to the great middle section of Luke, as well as to the birth and resurrection narratives, for distinctive features of the Gospel, although, to be sure, the sections where Luke more closely parallels the other Gospels also provide most pertinent insights for the understanding of his witness to Christ.

LUKE AND ACTS

Since in this study we are specifically dealing with the Gospel according to Luke, and have in view the evaluation of the distinctive place which it occupies in the Gospel canon, it might appear that little or no attention would have to be paid to The Acts. But the student of Luke would certainly fail to take due advantage of his exegetical assets if the single authorship and other relations

[1] See F. Kenyon, *Our Bible and the Ancient Manuscripts*, 1940, p. 10.

of the two writings were not kept constantly in mind. The Acts brings before us, anonymously and somewhat abruptly, but none the less definitely, the figure of a companion of Paul who is indisputably most significantly connected with the origin of the Acts, and is regarded by most scholars as unmistakably the real author of Luke-Acts. In addition to this testimony as to the origin of the Lucan writings, the Acts provides specific testimony as to the scope and disposition of the Gospel. In the opening sentence, the 'former treatise' is characterized as having to do with 'all that Jesus began both to do and teach until the day he was taken up.' Besides such pertinent information regarding the origin and contents of Luke, the Acts offers a treasury of data concerning Lucan vocabulary and usage which are of incalculable benefit for the interpreter of this Gospel.

No doubt these considerations are commonly recognized and utilized by students of Luke. But not less significant is the consideration, not so widely recognized, that Luke and Acts constitute a single work rather than two independently conceived writings.[1] This conclusion is based chiefly upon a study of the prefaces of Luke and Acts in comparison with prefaces in literary works of that era. Within a single literary work consisting of a number of divisions, writers were wont to utilize the device of prefaces of various sorts to indicate the scope and progress of their undertakings. Josephus, for example, in his work *Against Apion* begins with an extensive preface in which he reviews the ground covered in his monumental historical work, the *Antiquities*, and then intimates the purpose in view in his special treatise written as an answer to charges made against the Jewish people:

> 'I suppose that, by my book concerned with our antiquity, most excellent Epaphroditus, I have made it sufficiently evident to those who peruse them that our Jewish nation is of very great antiquity, and had a distinct subsistence of its own originally; and how we came to inhabit this country in which we now live. Those *Antiquities* contain the history of five thousand years, and are composed by me in Greek on the basis of our sacred books. However, since I observe a considerable number

[1] Cf. Zahn, *Einleitung in das N.T.*, 1907, II, Par. 60, note 10; Cadbury, *The Beginnings of Christianity*, Part I, Vol. II, pp. 489 f.; the same, *The Making of Luke-Acts*, 1927, pp. 194 ff.; Creed, *The Gospel according to St. Luke*, 1930, ad loc.

of people giving ear to the reproaches that are laid against us by those who bear ill-will to us, and do not believe what I have written concerning the antiquity of our nation, while they take it for a plain sign that our nation is of a later date, because it was not counted worthy of a bare mention by the most famous historiographers among the Grecians, I therefore have thought myself under an obligation to write somewhat briefly about all these subjects in order to refute the spite and voluntary falsehood of those that reproach us, and to correct the ignorance of others, and withal to instruct all those who are desirous of knowing the truth concerning our antiquity . . .'

At the beginning of Book II, Josephus introduces his discussion with a preface of much more restricted character, which is offered to apprise his readers of the progress he has made and the scope of that which is to come:

> 'In the former book, most honoured Epaphroditus, I have demonstrated our antiquity, and confirmed the truth of what I have said from the writings of the Phoenicians, and Chaldeans, and Egyptians. I have moreover produced many of the Grecian writers as witnesses thereto . . . I shall now therefore begin a refutation of the remaining authors who have written anything against us . . .'[1]

That the prefaces of Luke and the Acts, similarly, are essentially different from each other, and that the latter appropriately is subordinate to the more comprehensive preface at the commencement of the Gospel becomes clear. If Luke conceived of the Acts as a quite independent undertaking, and if, as would necessarily follow, Lk. i. 1-4 were intended as a preface merely to the Gospel, one would expect a somewhat similar preface at the beginning of the Acts. Since, however, a resumé of the first work is formulated and then the scope of the second portion is intimated, it cannot be doubted that the author intends to associate the Acts in a most intimate fashion with his earlier composition, and even to indicate that the Acts forms a second portion of a single undertaking in view at the very beginning.

To this line of argument it has been objected that the Acts does not set forth the scope of the second volume in specific terms, and

[1] The translations are largely from Whiston.

that therefore Luke could not have designed the opening words of the Acts, in imitation of literary practice, as a subordinate preface. The scope of the second volume is indeed not stated precisely and this argument is therefore not without weight. Nevertheless, it is intimated with sufficient clearness that the Acts has to do with the activity of the ascended Christ through the Holy Spirit, whom He was to pour out upon those who were to bear witness beginning from Jerusalem. At any rate a decisive consideration is found in the manner in which the writer takes stock of the ground covered in the previous volume before he proceeds with his narration of the unfolding of the new epoch with which the Acts is concerned.

If, however, the view that Luke and Acts constitute a single work is to be established on the basis of a true evaluation of the prefatory material, the Lucan preface in the four opening verses of the Gospel must be shown to possess the comprehensive character which, as has been intimated, commonly obtains in the case of prefaces at the beginning of a work of more than one volume. While perhaps the view that Luke and Acts are parts of a single work does not depend solely for support on the evidence that Lk. i. 1-4 applies to the whole work, and not merely to the Gospel, yet the demonstration of the pertinency of the Lucan prologue to the whole would go far in the direction of establishing it. This can be shown only on the basis of a careful examination of the prologue, and we shall turn to that task in the following chapter. But here we may anticipate the conclusion that, in our judgment, positive confirmation is forthcoming, and that, therefore, we cannot escape the fact that there must be constant reckoning with the Acts in our study of Luke.

It will appear that the conjunction with the Acts places this Gospel in the perspective of the history of Christianity. Whether, in common with the other evangelists, Luke is dealing with the historical career of Jesus Christ, or whether he is concentrating on his work as historian of the founding of the Christian Church, he is treating a single theme. His theme is Jesus Christ. More particularly he aims to deal with the action of Jesus Christ, both in word and deed, as He once for all laid the foundations of Christianity. The living Lord of the Church is the same as the person who lived as a man among men. The Jesus who is portrayed as being Himself led of the Holy Spirit is the One whose effusion of the Holy Spirit from on high brought the Church into existence and who through His bestowal of the Spirit continued to manifest His gracious rule of and on behalf of the Church.

But Luke is not so much under the spell of the unity of his theme that he obscures the diversity of its manifestation. The ascension of Christ draws a firm line between the two segments of that history, and so the career on earth stands apart in sharp contrast with the heavenly ministry of the ascended Lord. Though the Gospel was not written as bare history, isolated from the faith of the writer and of the Christian Church, yet it was set down as that which actually occurred. The contrasts between the Acts and the Gospel demonstrate that Luke had a strong historical sense. He was far from supposing that the story which he narrated in the Gospel had been transformed by the developing faith of the early Christians.

LUKE THE AUTHOR

The question of the identity of the author of the Third Gospel is not of basic importance in these studies since the first and last concern is with meaning rather than origins. Nevertheless, since Luke is, strictly speaking, not an anonymous work, and the original readers, at least, must have been influenced in their evaluation of its message by their thoughts concerning the qualifications of the author, brief treatment of this question will be advantageous.

That all the church fathers who have left us testimony on this point agree in ascribing both the Gospel and Acts to Luke, who is frequently identified as a companion of Paul, is clearly of the utmost significance. The testimony of the fathers is indeed not particularly early, for Irenaeus (*c.* A.D. 185) offers apparently the first extant witness. However, the evidence represented by the superscription in the Gospel manuscripts reflects the recognition of Lucan authorship several decades earlier.[1] Since a very large part of Luke's claim to distinction rests upon the association of his name with Luke-Acts, the tradition gives a *prima facie* impression of owing its origin to accurate information.

[1] Cf. J. H. Ropes, *The Synoptic Gospels*, 1934, pp. 102 f., where it is argued that the Gospel titles must date from about A.D. 125. The testimony of the Lucan Anti-Marcionite Prologue (probably A.D. 160–180) is also significant.

Owing to the undisputed unity of authorship of Luke and Acts, this Gospel has the advantage of a broader base of internal testimony than the others. The 'we'-sections in Acts, as Irenaeus himself argued, show that Luke was inseparable from Paul and present at all the occurrences narrated therein.[1] It is generally admitted today that the author of the 'we'-sections was a companion of Paul. And most if not all who deny the Lucan authorship of Luke-Acts are sufficiently impressed by the historical tradition to allow that that companion must have been Luke. But in modern times there has been widespread doubt as to the correctness of identifying the author of the complete work with the author, or 'diarist,' of the sections which employ the first person plural.[2]

Harnack, who had shared this negative position, created a minor sensation when he became a vigorous advocate of the traditional view. He argued effectively that there is an accumulation of Lucan linguistic characteristics in these sections, which is understandable when one considers that the author of Luke-Acts would here be his own reporter, and thus not influenced by the linguistic peculiarities of sources.[3]

Though the arguments of Harnack and various allies have convinced many scholars, there have been others who have remained unpersuaded. Windisch, for example, has vigorously presented 'The Case Against The Tradition'[4] and Cadbury has argued that the tradition may be merely an inference from certain data in Luke-Acts (such as the prefaces and the 'we' references) and from such a statement as 2 Tim. iv. 11 ('Only Luke is with me').[5]

The decision necessarily turns largely about the evaluation of the 'we'-sections. Windisch does not of course base his negative judgment upon the supposition that the use of 'we' is the literary

[1] *Adv. Haer.* III, xiv. 1.

[2] The sections are Acts xvi. 10–17 (or 18); xx. 5–xxi. 26 (cf. verse 18); xxvii. 1–xxviii. 16. In addition, the western text of Acts xi. 28 contains the phrase 'when we were gathered together', and thus places the anonymous companion at Antioch.

[3] Cf. *Luke the Physician*, 1906 (Eng. Trans. 1907); *The Acts of the Apostles*, 1908 (Eng. Trans. 1909); *The Date of the Acts and of the Synoptic Gospels*, 1911. J. C. Hawkins, *Horae Synopticae*, 2nd edit., 1909, pp. 182 ff. is also important.

[4] In *The Beginnings of Christianity*, Part I, Vol. II, pp. 304 ff., 343 f.

[5] *Making of Luke-Acts*, pp. 353 ff.

fiction of a writer who, though far from the historic scene, sought to give the impression that he was writing his treatise with the qualifications of an eye-witness. For if he were trying to convey such an impression, he would have used the device far more pervasively than he has done. One would indeed have a problem on one's hands if it were necessary to account for the restraint in which virtual claims of eye-witnessship are made if they are pure inventions. Windisch's argument rather takes the line that the author of Acts used a diary which originally came from Luke. That the author and the diarist are not to be identified follows especially, he maintains, from the consideration that we should otherwise expect him to explain his sudden appearances and disappearances. Cadbury similarly is impressed with the 'abrupt and unexplained "we"' and considers the problem posed by these literary phenomena 'an insoluble riddle.'

Are the appearances and disappearances as abrupt and sudden, however, as is supposed? And can we rightly demand that the author-diarist ought to have informed his readers more particularly as to his own movements? Clearly the diary was used intelligently, with due regard to situation and sequence. The anonymous companion does not turn up in surprising places: he first appears as Paul is about to go to Philippi; he remains behind in that city when Paul leaves; he joins Paul at the apostle's next visit to Philippi and accompanies him to Jerusalem; for a time he evidently goes his own way, but is again found in Paul's company on the journey from Palestine to Rome. And though he takes account of his own presence at certain phases of Paul's career, he quite deliberately, and in accordance with the inconspicuous character of his own role, keeps himself in the background. To have dwelt upon the reasons why he stayed behind in Philippi the first time, and why he accompanied Paul the second time, and did not remain with Paul during his entire stay in Jerusalem would have shifted the centre of interest, at least to some extent, from Paul to himself. One can understand that a modest companion of the great apostle would have been determined to avoid distracting the attention of his readers from Paul to himself. In short, the unobtrusive way in which the first person plural is utilized contributes to the total effect without allowing the work to become autobiographical.

If the supposedly unknown author of Luke-Acts decided to make use of a diary of Luke, one might claim that this is simply another instance of the use of sources which were available to him. But why then did the author not employ this source as he does other sources? Why did he clumsily retain the 'we' of his source? It is in attempting to answer this question that Windisch most openly displays the basic weakness of his own position. His answer, in a word, is that it can be accounted for by the literary methods of antiquity, and that 'the same naïveté which impels the author of Acts to leave the "we" of another's diary which he incorporates into his own history appears elsewhere, when he attributes speeches which he himself invented or elaborated to Peter, Gamaliel, Stephen, or Paul.'[1] However, even if it were granted that the speeches were composed by the author of Acts,[2] Windisch's point with regard to the 'we'-phenomena would not be well taken. As Windisch himself says, the former would today be regarded as 'deception.' But the retention of 'we' in no sense involves an ethical question; it is a purely literary matter, and would warrant the charge of extreme clumsiness. And it is exactly this charge that would be virtually indefensible in the light of the accumulation of evidence of the extraordinary literary skill of the author of Luke-Acts. This is pointedly true in the present instance because, on the assumption that author and diarist are not identical, it would have to be admitted that the very author who had clumsily retained 'we' had for the rest conformed the 'we' sections linguistically to his own language and style.[3]

It appears actually that those scholars who still today reject the tradition of Lucan authorship are far more basically influenced by doctrinal and historical judgments than by literary considerations. Windisch specifically states that 'the so-called "lower criticism" is never able . . . to maintain itself against "higher criticism",' and his case against the tradition is seen to consist largely of arguments to the effect that 'the Lucan Paul is not consistent with

[1] Op. cit., p. 343.

[2] On the authenticity of the speeches, cf. F. F. Bruce, *The Speeches in the Acts*, Tyndale Press, London, 1942.

[3] Cf. Creed, op. cit., p. xiv, note 1. Cadbury states the difficulty (*Making*, etc., p. 358), but does not overcome it.

the Paul of the authentic Epistles.'[1] Cadbury agrees that a main issue is 'whether the treatment of Paul's visits to Jerusalem, especially that of Acts xv with its decrees, is too unhistorical to have emanated from one who later was Paul's associate,' but concludes that we are here carried 'into realms where our information is quite insufficient for secure judgment.'[2] Creed analyses the situation similarly, and finds certain 'historical improbabilities' in Acts, but evidently judges that there is nothing that disproves Lucan authorship.[3] It is fortunate that on these basic matters one may appeal to the thorough and satisfying treatment given by Machen.[4]

The exceedingly weighty evidence of the 'we' sections does not indeed establish the Lucan authorship of Luke-Acts. Its corroboration of the tradition does not go beyond proving that the author was a companion of Paul. However, the significance of this conclusion should not be underestimated. There is, for example, nothing in Matthew or Mark comparable to this internal testimony. And in the modern discussion of the origins of the Gospels the central question is not precisely that of authorship so much as that of the nearness of the authors to the events which they narrate. If the diarist was the author of Luke-Acts, he was a person who not only knew Paul intimately but also had abundant opportunities for establishing intimate contact with other leading figures of the Christian Church including James (Acts xxi. 18) and Philip (Acts xxi. 8-12). Not merely the tradition of Lucan authorship, therefore, but also the testimony of Luke-Acts itself supports the judgment that the work owes its origin, not to one who was out of touch with the persons and events he describes, but to one who himself visited Jerusalem within three decades of the death of our Lord, and had splendid opportunities of becoming intimately acquainted with many of the earliest and best-informed Christians.

There are other considerations, moreover, which, though not positively identifying the author as Luke, are highly congruous

[1] Op. cit., p. 344; p. 317; pp. 321 ff.

[2] *Making*, p. 357.

[3] Op. cit. pp. xv f.

[4] In *The Origin of Paul's Religion*, 1921, pp. 37 ff. 43 ff., 71 ff. The answer of B. H. Streeter, *The Four Gospels*, 1930, pp. 543 ff., 548 f., note 1, is also of special interest.

with the tradition, and possess a certain cumulative force in substantiation of it.[1] The author of this work has chosen to introduce himself only as an anonymous companion of Paul on certain sections of his missionary journeys, and therefore such companions as Timothy, Silas and Aristarchus, who are mentioned in Acts, may not be regarded as candidates for the honour. On the other hand, Luke, though otherwise evidently well-known, remains unmentioned. The same might be said of Titus, but Luke has every advantage over him since Titus does not appear in those Epistles of Paul evidently written in the period introduced by the conclusion of Acts. Luke, however, is present as an intimate fellow-worker of Paul (Phm. 24; Col. iv. 14; cf. 2 Tim. iv. 11). This fact is important, not only because, if Luke is the author, Acts and Paul would agree in placing Luke in Rome in Paul's company, but also because the several concluding chapters of Acts suggest that their author was a person who was in intimate touch with Paul and was especially concerned with the critical events leading to his arrest. It is also of interest that Luke is not mentioned in the Thessalonian Epistles nor in the Corinthian and Roman Epistles, and this is exactly what one would expect if the diarist was Luke. For the former were written on the second missionary journey after Paul had left him behind in Macedonia; and the latter evidently on the third journey before he joined Paul at Acts xx. 4 for the trip to Jerusalem.

There are a few other facts concerning Luke which accord well with the tradition. Luke's acquaintance with Mark is intimated by Paul (Col. iv. 10, 14; Phm. 24), and the author was obviously remarkably well-informed concerning Mark's life, even to the point of knowing the name of the maid in his mother's home in Jerusalem (cf. Acts xii. 12, 25, xiii. 13, xv. 37 ff.). Luke was a Greek (cf. Col. iv. 14 and iv. 10 f.), and the language is best understood on the supposition that the author was a Greek of considerable literary skill. Of still greater interest is Paul's designation of Luke as 'the beloved physician' (Col. iv. 14). Following the monumental study of Hobart, such students of Luke as Plummer, Zahn and Harnack have acknowledged that Luke-Acts displays various medical traits and interests that confirm the tradition that

[1] Windisch, op. cit., pp. 315 f., admits that such considerations as follow are 'strong arguments in favour of the correctness of the tradition.'

its author was a physician.[1] This contention has been subjected to a very severe criticism by Cadbury, who supports the charge that the whole argument is 'an immense fallacy.'[2] More recently, however, Creed has observed that, though the argument as originally stated was exaggerated, there has, on the other hand, been an undue depreciation of the force of the medical parallels. He also presents the timely reminder that the final question is not whether the medical language establishes the conclusion that the author was a physician, but whether it contributes corroboration of the tradition.[3]

These several considerations taken singly would perhaps be of relatively little weight, but together they possess cumulative force of a high order when one takes due account of the strength of the early Christian tradition of Lucan authorship. If such considerations as these pointed much more definitely to Luke as the author than they actually do, the argument might lose much of its weight. For then one might perhaps argue with some plausibility that the tradition was an inference from these data. The true situation is, however, that early Christian tradition unanimously and confidently assigns the work to Luke, who otherwise was not remembered as an influential member of the Christian community, and that in a very incidental and unobtrusive fashion the New Testament exhibits the congruity and tenability of the tradition. As the prefaces of Luke and Acts show with particular clarity, Luke-Acts is not strictly speaking an anonymous work. And the first readers would surely have been apprised of the identity of the author. Hence there would have been from very early times a Christian tradition as to the author. If this person was some one other than Luke, his name and connection with the work must have disappeared completely from view at a very early time, and were replaced by the allegedly fictitious tradition of Lucan authorship.

[1] Cf. W. K. Hobart, *The Medical Language of St. Luke*, 1882; A. Plummer, *The Gospel according to St. Luke* (ICC), 1896, pp. lxiii ff.; Zahn, op. cit., Par. 62 and note 5 (pp. 433 f.; 442 f.); Harnack, *Luke the Physician*, pp. 175 ff.

[2] Cf. *Beginnings*, etc., pp. 346 ff.; *Making*, etc., p. 219, p. 358; and especially *The Style and Literary Method of Luke*, 1920, pp. 39 ff.

[3] Op. cit., pp. xviii ff.

CRITICAL PERSPECTIVES

On the whole the tendencies of modern criticism have not enhanced the reputation of the third evangelist as an accurate and trustworthy narrator. For some the writings of Luke have never fully recovered from the attack of the Tübingen School. In spite of the almost universal rejection of its radical, Hegel-inspired, reconstruction of history, and of many of its judgments on detailed points, certain basic perspectives of this School remain influential. The conjecture of Baur that Luke was really a revision of Marcion's Gospel, and was first published as late as about the middle of the second century, did not hold the field for any considerable length of time. But his low view of Acts, based largely on alleged discrepancies with Paul's Epistles, has continued to be an important factor in recent criticism of the Lucan writings.[1]

The development of the Marcan Hypothesis, while itself representing a sharp divergence from the position of Baur, involved a depreciation of the right of Luke to be heard on its own merits. For the very act of elevating Mark to a position of priority and superiority to the other Gospels assigned Luke, along with Matthew, to a secondary rank. Nor has the incisive criticism of the Marcan Hypothesis associated with the names of Wrede and Wellhausen, and which forms a background for the development of Form-criticism, served substantially to increase respect for Luke. For this radical attack upon the historical worth of Mark has also presupposed the priority of Mark, and, except perhaps for certain aspects of the message of Jesus, the relative superiority of Mark to the other Gospels. The illuminating commentary of J. M. Creed, published in 1930, is typical of this tendency. While allowing that Luke may have had access to some literary sources and some historical tradition, he interprets Luke as in the main a consummate literary artist who freely adapted his sources to suit his ends and in all probability was himself responsible for the literary creation of a considerable part of his distinctive material.[2]

[1] Windisch's approach is rather typical of the modern revised and moderated form of the Tübingen approach. But Baur's thesis that Marcion's Canon largely influenced the formation of Luke-Acts has been sympathetically re-examined and restated by J. Knox, *Marcion and the New Testament*, 1942. See my review in WTJ, Nov. 1943, pp. 86 ff., 95 ff.

[2] Creed maintains, for example, that the preaching at Nazareth, the com-

A somewhat more conservative tendency is represented by the development of the four-document theory, which has gained considerable vogue as the result of the original work of Streeter and the support given by Taylor, Easton and W. Manson among others.[1] This approach is more conservative particularly in that most of the distinctively Lucan materials are regarded as having been in written form considerably before the evangelist published his Gospel, and as having a right accordingly to be weighed on their own merits as a source or sources independent of Mark. Although it is not an essential feature of this literary hypothesis that Luke was the author of Proto-Luke as well as of the finished Gospel, Streeter does maintain this position. Indeed, he concludes that Luke himself was active in collecting information and making copious notes during the last two years that he was in Caesarea in the company of Paul, and that he later combined these materials with 'Q' to form Proto-Luke. It is beyond the scope of our present undertaking to evaluate this hypothesis. And in calling attention to its 'conservative' character, my intention is not to imply that it offers a necessarily more satisfactory theory of Gospel origins than the two-document theory. Its multiplication of literary sources of a hypothetical nature, for example, does not commend it. And in continuing to approach the synoptic problem almost exclusively in terms of documents, it does not do justice to the factor of the oral proclamation of the Gospel. But there is a gratifying amount of historical realism in its evaluation of the situation in which Luke and the other Gospels came into existence. To a far greater extent than the prevalent forms of the two-document theory, it allows for the viewpoint that the distinctive testimony of Luke constitutes authentic tradition.

Mention must also be made here of the highly significant work of Cadbury. His approach is rather independent and therefore also somewhat difficult of classification. His major work on Luke, *The Making of Luke-Acts*, appeared in 1927, three years after the first edition of Streeter's *The Four Gospels*, and he

mission of the risen Lord, the Ascension, and Pentecost constitute free creations of the author's historical imagination, p. xviii. But Luke is also said to be conservative in his treatment of sources, pp. lxii, lxxi.

[1] Streeter, op. cit., V. Taylor, *Behind the Third Gospel*, 1926; B. S. Easton, *The Gospel according to St. Luke*, 1926; W. Manson, *The Gospel of Luke*, 1930.

expresses himself on Streeter's position, chiefly in footnotes, with reserve but somewhat favourably. In the main, however, his views seem to correspond more closely with the position which Creed was to set forth in his Commentary of 1930, although he places more emphasis upon the factor of Luke's environment—the materials which were available and the methods and standards of the time—and less upon the creative imagination of the author, than is true of Creed. But, as has been noted, Cadbury exceeds most modern students in the general agnosticism of his approach to the question of origins. And, in keeping with his emphasis upon the historical environment which he finds reflected in Luke-Acts, rather than upon the decisive influence of historic personalities, one gains the impression that this work is regarded as being a first-class witness only for the time and situation in which it came into existence. But as we shall see in our examination of the Prologue, and many other features of the Gospel, the modern student has been placed greatly in his debt both because of the learning and acuteness of many of his observations and because of the stimulus to fresh study which results from an evaluation of his theories.

It will be recognized that the foregoing review of opinion does not aim at comprehensiveness. Like the other materials in this introductory chapter, it will have accomplished the end in view if the summary and selective treatment has succeeded in indicating perspectives which may profitably be kept in mind as one examines the witness of the Gospel. These perspectives are of immediate moment as one reflects upon the testimony of the prologue.

CHAPTER II

CHRISTIANITY ACCORDING TO THE PROLOGUE

EASILY the most specific testimony which Luke provides for the understanding of his own evaluation of his work is afforded by the stately and meaningful sentence with which he begins his Gospel. Although he takes only one sentence to enunciate what he is undertaking to do, this sentence of more than forty words is so weighty in its declarations and implications that it commands minute and painstaking examination. Here at the very beginning, determined to leave no doubt as to his qualifications, methods and goal, the author makes a personal bow to his readers. Except for this statement the Gospel might be regarded as an anonymous work. We should take care, indeed, not to base our conclusions as to Luke's claims exclusively upon the prologue, for that would be as foolhardy as to judge an architect's design solely from the blueprints after the completed building has been opened to inspection. The Gospel as it lies before us, and the Acts as well, must be allowed to tell all that they have to testify concerning what Luke evidently intended to accomplish. Nevertheless, it would be difficult to exaggerate the distinctive contribution which is made to our knowledge of the origin of Luke-Acts by the opening words.

The prologue is of special significance today from a different point of view. Although its chief interest lies in what the author tells in advance concerning himself and his undertaking, the fact remains that this information is set forth against a background of activity by certain predecessors. And what Luke says concerning these predecessors provides us with a most valuable testimony concerning a crucial, but not too well known, period of Christian history. This is the period between the ascension of Christ and the commencement of the documentation of Christianity, the period of close on twenty years before the earliest Epistles were written, of perhaps thirty years or more before the earliest Gospel was published. These writings of the New Testament supply us with all our certain historical information concerning the career of Christ. They also directly and indirectly light up the earliest days of the

Christian church. It may not be overlooked, however, that the gospel of Jesus Christ was handed down *orally*, at least for the most part, during the first decades. And one may quite legitimately be concerned with that earliest phase of the proclamation of the gospel which forms the background for its commitment to writing.

The method of Form-criticism, which has come to the fore since the close of the first World War, has centred attention upon this period and has sought to explain the origins of the Gospels in terms of the developing faith and life of the early Christian communities. Its historical presuppositions and critical methods are open to weighty objections, and it is radically astray in its central evaluation of Christianity and its writings as being more fundamentally the product of social forces than the realization of the purposes of Jesus Christ. But it has the merit of centring attention upon the significance of this period for our understanding of Christianity and acknowledging oral tradition as a basic factor in the formation of the Gospels.[1] Luke's prologue, to be sure, is not oriented to the modern critical situation, but he does have some significant things to say concerning developments in this period. He deserves to be considered more fully and earnestly by those who are dealing with the subject of the formation of the gospel tradition.

LUKE'S PREDECESSORS

Luke's characterization of the work of his predecessors may conveniently be discussed under the following heads: (1) the facts with which they were concerned; (2) the transmission of these facts; and (3) the beginnings of the composition of documents.

The subject matter with which Luke's predecessors dealt is described in an arresting phrase, translated in the Revised Version with apparent matter-of-factness as 'those matters which have been fulfilled among us', but with somewhat greater force in the margin by those matters which have been 'fully established' among us. More religiously colourful is the familiar language of the Authorized Version, 'those things which are most surely believed among us,' but this quality does not justify the translation.

[1] For analysis and criticism of *Formgeschichte*, see articles and reviews in WTJ, 1938-39, pp. 13 ff.; 1939-40, pp. 110 ff., 135 ff.; 1943-44, pp. 200 ff.

The verb may, indeed, mean to *convince* or *persuade*; it is thus used several times by Paul in the passive voice, as for example in Rom. xiv. 5: 'Let each man be fully persuaded in his own mind.' But this meaning can hardly stand here for, though persons may be persuaded, things cannot.[1]

The meaning of the verb: *to fulfil, establish*, or *accomplish* (cf. 2 Tim. iv. 5, 17), on the other hand, completely satisfies the Greek construction. Renderings in the direction of the Revision of 1881, therefore, are definitely more acceptable than the translation of the Authorized Version of 1611. It should not be lost sight of, however, that the verb used here is not the word ordinarily translated by 'fulfil,' as for example in Lk. iv. 21, where our Lord says, 'Today hath this Scripture been fulfilled in your ears.' Perhaps the rarer Greek word has been chosen for merely formal reasons because of the literary interest of Luke. Blass, who has helpfully dealt with the language and style of the prologue, and speaks of it as 'a very remarkable specimen of fine and well-balanced structure, and at the same time of well-chosen vocabulary,' explains this and other terms as being selected because they are 'grander and sonorous.'[2] Although, accordingly, the word chosen does not necessarily connote more than the more common, simpler verb 'fulfil' in various contexts where divine or human plans are spoken of as being accomplished, yet the use of this unusual word does centre attention upon the Lucan philosophy of history. According to Luke's understanding the matters accomplished were of such a character that they did not somehow accomplish themselves in the onrush of the stream of history. For in Acts i. 1 he sums up the Gospel as being concerned with what *Jesus* began to do and teach, and in the total perspective of Luke-Acts Jesus is viewed as the divine Lord who through His

[1] Eusebius (*H.E.* III, xxiv. 15) also seems to have been influenced by this meaning of the verb, for he declares that Luke explains that many others had somewhat rashly undertaken to compose a narrative of the things of which 'he himself had acquired full assurance' or, 'he himself had been brought to conviction' (αὐτὸς πεπληροφόρητο λόγων). But no special weight should be attached to Eusebius' interpretation since evidently it is based upon his imperfect memory of the prologue rather than upon a careful consideration of what Luke actually said. Luke is clearly speaking of his predecessors rather than of himself at this point.

[2] *The Philology of the Gospels*, 1898, pp. 7, 12. See also Cadbury, *Beginnings of Christianity*, I, ii. 1922, p. 496: 'a longer and more sonorous word'.

presence upon earth and through the agency of the Holy Spirit after His ascension accomplished the divine plan.[1]

The events fulfilled 'among us,' that is, in the midst of the Christian community in Palestine, were accordingly thought of as being far from ordinary. They were in short a series of events, intimately associated with respect to time and place, having taken place within a brief epoch in Palestine; events of a public or semi-public nature, having occurred in the midst of the life of men ('among us'), and of epochal meaning for the life of the Christian church. As the Gospel makes clear, these events are the facts of foundational significance for the Church, including especially the birth, the death and the resurrection of Jesus Christ. Though these events are viewed as belonging to the past, the choice of the perfect tense confirms the impression that they are thought of as being of abiding significance.

We proceed now to examine what Luke has to say on the timely question of the transmission of knowledge concerning the foundational facts to the point of documentation in the writings of his predecessors. This period of transmission obviously cannot be marked off sharply as a precisely delineated interval between the occurrence of the events and the preparation of written records. For significant events took place after the transmission of a knowledge of other events had begun and probably even after the earliest composition of documents. Nevertheless, the great events of the Gospel belonged to the past when their communication to the church began.

Of primary interest is the question as to the persons who, according to Luke, were responsible for the transmission of this knowledge of what had taken place. Luke describes them as those 'who from the beginning were eyewitnesses and ministers of the word.'[2] The task of identifying the eyewitnesses and ministers is advanced considerably when one observes that Luke evidently has only one group of persons in view rather than two. Perhaps the most conclusive proof that Luke is not distinguishing eyewitnesses from ministers of the word is the use of the single

[1] Cf. also Cadbury, *Making*, pp. 303 f. and O. Piper, 'The Purpose of Luke', in *Union Seminary Review*, Nov. 1945 (LVII), pp. 15 ff.

[2] So rendered in RV; similarly in AV and RSV.

predicate 'handed down' (παρέδοσαν) with the compound subject, which alone explains why Luke introduces his reference to this company of persons here; it is their activity in transmitting a knowledge of certain events which is the connecting link between the occurrence of the events and the literary activity of Luke's predecessors. Two different groups of persons could indeed be engaged in this single activity, but, whereas ministers of the word would as such necessarily *transmit* information, eyewitnesses would as such only *receive* it. Hence, Luke includes the term eyewitnesses, not to designate a separate group, but in order to call attention to the historical qualification of these ministers of the word to transmit the facts. The conclusion that Luke has only one group of persons in mind receives confirmation, moreover, from the participial construction which, employing a single article, serves to join together the persons designated by the nouns into one close-knit group. Finally, there are sound reasons for construing the phrase 'from the beginning' with the participle, rather than merely with the noun 'eyewitnesses,' and this provides another indication that Luke is referring to the *original* company of qualified persons, the eyewitness-ministers, who were responsible for the transmission of 'the things fulfilled among us.'[1]

If, therefore, the group responsible for the transmission of the facts is the original company of qualified persons, the earliest eyewitnesses and first preachers, who can Luke have specifically in mind but the apostles and perhaps a few of their associates? In my judgment all possible remaining doubt that Luke has the apostolic circle pointedly in view is removed when account is taken of the clear distinction drawn between this group and Luke's predecessors. If these predecessors, and evidently Luke himself as a later associate (at least so far as the Gospel facts are concerned), are viewed as dependent upon the eyewitness-ministers, Luke cannot be thinking of this group as loosely comprehending a

[1] Acts xxvi. 4, illustrates the propriety of construing the prepositional phrase with the participle. 'From the beginning' has appropriate reference to 'eyewitnesses,' indicating their qualification to witness to things fulfilled from the beginning (cf. Acts i. 21 f., x. 37), but this is not a reason for restricting its reference to 'eyewitnesses.' See also Cadbury, *Beginnings*, I, ii, p. 498.

The aorist tense of the participle points to the qualification possessed by the original company of eyewitness-ministers to transmit knowledge to Luke's predecessors; it does not imply that they were no longer active when the prologue was written.

broad circle of disciples of the apostles or younger contemporaries.[1]

This conclusion is of far-reaching significance for the evaluation of the subject of the origins of the Gospels. In the present century, as has been noted, criticism has tended to view the gospel as basically a social product and the Gospels as theological creations of the Christian community. The Gospels were indeed written by believing members of the Christian church and were written to meet actual needs which existed at the time of their composition. But they can be regarded as social products only if the distinctive place occupied by Jesus Christ, and that filled by His immediate disciples, is radically discounted and obscured. Certainly, if Luke's testimony is taken at all seriously, such views must be set aside. According to the testimony of the prologue, the community is not even viewed as the principal agent for the transmission of the tradition, much less as responsible for its origin and formulation. Rather Luke intimates that there was a small well-defined group of persons who had been in immediate touch with the events and who had special authority and responsibility for their earliest proclamation. That Luke actually attached unique significance to the apostolic preaching is abundantly confirmed by the place assigned to the apostles' testimony in the early chapters of Acts. It was the apostles who 'went in and went out among us, beginning from the baptism of John unto the day that he was received up from us,' and thus were qualified to preach the message which found its climax in the resurrection of Jesus.[2]

Concerning the form in which Luke's predecessors received their information we learn nothing definite from the prologue. Since the verb 'handed down' could be used of transmission through written documents (as in Acts vi. 14 where reference is made to 'the customs which Moses delivered to us'), we cannot exclude the possibility that some of the tradition to which Luke refers may have been in written form. Nevertheless, there can be little doubt that oral tradition is chiefly, if not exclusively, in view. Luke appears to draw a contrast between those who like himself (the 'many') were concerned to compose a narrative in

[1] Cadbury's distinctive view is considered below.

[2] Cf. Acts i. 22, ii. 42, vi. 4, and the record of the apostolic preaching which is a conspicuous feature of the Acts.

written form and the company of persons who, by their oral proclamation of the things which they had seen and heard, provided the materials for such literary works.[1]

The only other information Luke provides concerning these early documents is found in his intimation that 'many' had been engaged in such literary efforts. The general tendency of modern interpreters is to discount this detail as being a conventional feature of a largely conventional preface. This is the position, for example, of Cadbury and Dibelius. And Streeter thinks that Mark must have been mainly in view but that the 'vague and general' mention of 'many' was employed in order that readers brought up on Mark could not have their feelings hurt.[2] In my judgment, however, there is nothing improbable in the view that by the sixth decade of the first century several attempts had been made in the various churches to provide written accounts of the apostolic preaching and teaching. The need which Mark and Luke supplied, for example, may well have been felt previously in many churches. To suppose, however, that several such compositions came into existence prior to Luke's literary activity does not imply that they were generally as comprehensive as our canonical Gospels or that they were ever regarded as possessing the authority and competence of our Gospels. Even quite provisional and fairly brief written formulations of the apostolic

[1] Blass, op. cit., pp. 15 ff. appeals to the use of the verb in Plutarch and Irenaeus to substantiate the rendering 'to restore from memory,' and concludes that Luke has in mind the restoration of oral tradition from living memory. However, the data appear to be too meagre to warrant a dogmatic conclusion. Moreover, in the use of this verb by Irenaeus (*Adv. Haer.* III xxi. 2) it is well to observe that, though Ezra is described as having 'reconstructed from memory' what the ancient writer had composed, and therefore as having depended on his memory of tradition, the fact remains that the tradition in view is regarded as having existed originally in written form before it was lost. So even if Blass's rendering could be insisted upon, this fact would not be decisive for the determination of the original form of the tradition. See also Creed, ad loc.

[2] Cadbury, *Beginnings*, I. ii, pp. 492 f.; Dibelius, *Gospel Criticism and Christology*, 1935, pp. 30 f.; Streeter, *The Four Gospels*, p. 559. On the other hand, Harnack, *Date of the Acts*, p. 125 n., in connection with his support of the early dating of Luke, declares that 'with our complete ignorance of the circumstances it is quite inadmissible for us any longer so to tie ourselves down to one decade as to say that a decade later there were "many" that could have written, while a decade earlier there could not have been many.' F. W. Grosheide, 'The Synoptic Problem' in EQ, January 1931, takes the reference to 'many' quite literally, but supposes that oral Gospels are in view.

preaching would have qualified under the terms Luke applies to the works of his predecessors.

DOES LUKE DISPARAGE HIS PREDECESSORS?

If Luke's direct testimony as to his qualifications, methods and goal is to be placed in its correct perspective, it will be essential to gauge his evaluation of the work of his predecessors in relation to his own. One question at issue here is whether he had a favourable or an unfavourable view of their efforts. Eusebius definitely took the latter view, for he states that Luke explains that 'since many others had *rather rashly attempted* to compose a narrative of the things of which he himself had acquired full assurance, and feeling the necessity of freeing us from *the doubtful opinions of the others*, he delivered in his own Gospel the accurate account of the things of which he had firmly apprehended the truth . . . being aided by his association and contact with Paul and his conversation with the remaining apostles.'[1] But the antiquity of this interpretation is about all that can be said in its favour, for it varies at several points from what Luke actually says. Evidently Eusebius is depending on his memory rather than upon actual examination of the text of Luke, and hence gives a very free paraphrase rather than an accurate exegesis.

If careful account is taken of what Luke actually says, it will appear that there is no real support for the view that he is depreciating the work of his predecessors. On the contrary, his general characterizations of their qualifications and actions create at least a presumption in favour of the view that he means to acknowledge their positive worth. In fact, when the language of the opening two verses (the protasis) is compared with that of the final two (the apodosis), it appears that the parallelism is so pervasive that virtually all that he says about them he might as well have said concerning himself.

One should observe, first of all, that the use of the verb 'undertaken' in describing their efforts by no means implies disparagement. If it is translated 'attempted,' it might indeed imply that Luke intended to do what others had tried but failed to carry out satisfactorily. But such a derogatory connotation

[1] H.E., III, xxiv. 15. Cf. note [1], p. 26, above.

finds no positive basis in the use of this verb. As Moulton and Milligan indicate on the background of their examination of various instances of the use of this verb in non-literary Hellenistic Greek, 'any idea of failure, though often suggested by the context, does not lie in the verb itself.'

And in the context Luke makes clear that he mentions them, not to discount or disparage them, but to indicate that he is not engaged in a novel enterprise. He says, 'it seemed good *to me also* to write . . .' He thereby associates himself in the most intimate manner with those who had undertaken to draw up a narrative.

In harmony with this approach Luke implies that he occupies essentially the same ground as his predecessors with regard to subject matter, the transmission of information, and literary aim. The subject matter is quite the same. When he says that they dealt with 'the things fulfilled among us,' he clearly has in view the events which were of immediate concern to, and one might say also the common property of, the entire Christian church, including Luke just as much as the 'many.' Moreover, he regards them as possessing the same happy relation to the facts as he. This is borne out by what he has to say in verse 2 concerning the agents of the transmission of the facts and their actual interest in a faithful transmission of them. The many have undertaken to compose an account of the things fulfilled among us 'just as those who from the beginning were eyewitnesses and ministers of the word delivered them unto us.' Accordingly, they as well as he were dependent upon the original company of eyewitness-ministers, not upon persons whose connection with the history was more tenuous. And they, too, were concerned to see that their accounts constituted a fair representation of the matter that was handed down. In view of Luke's intimate and respectful association of himself with his predecessors, it follows that the testimony concerning them bears very pointedly upon the question of his estimation of his own work.

LUKE'S SELF-TESTIMONY

We turn now to an evaluation of Luke's own direct characterization of his work as set forth in the final two verses of the prologue. We shall note what he has to say concerning (1) the subject matter of his undertaking, (2) his own relation to the facts, and (3) the orderliness and goal of his composition.

One is impressed at once with the comprehensiveness of Luke's investigation, for he states that he was concerned with 'all things.' The scope of his own endeavour is, accordingly, hardly more restricted than that of his predecessors who had been occupied with 'the things fulfilled among us.' Luke states somewhat more precisely what his subject matter is when he formulates his goal as that of providing Theophilus with certainty concerning the things wherein he was instructed. Regardless of the decisions reached on other matters relating to Theophilus, such as the question whether or not he was a Christian (a problem which will be considered below), we may affirm without hesitation that the information conveyed to him had to do with the origin and progress of Christianity.

These data bear significantly upon the question whether the prologue comprehends in its perspective the book of Acts as well as the Gospel. Even the general description of Luke's subject matter found in the prologue hardly permits of restriction to the events prior to the ascension of Christ. Theophilus could hardly have remained totally uninformed, even on the earliest plausible dating of Luke's writings, concerning those momentous happenings after the departure of Christ, such as the outpouring of the Spirit at Pentecost, which were of decisive significance for the spread of Christianity.

Luke is most personal when he informs us of his special qualifications to write. It seemed good to him to write, he says, 'having followed all things accurately from the first.' The participle translated 'having followed' is rendered more impressively in the Revised Version as 'having traced the course of' all things. Although the basic meaning of the verb 'follow' is not to be lost sight of, neither should the rich significance of Luke's claims remain unappreciated. Modernization must be avoided; Luke did not operate as a modern scholar carrying on historical research. Nevertheless, the verb 'follow' in this context, concerned as it is with the pursuit of knowledge of historical facts, and being directed to the examination of sources of information, means essentially 'to acquire familiarity with' all things. Accordingly, investigation is definitely implied in the use of the verb 'follow,' even though it may not have been conducted precisely like that of a twentieth-century scholar.[1]

We observe, therefore, that Luke's comprehensive inquiry into the history of Christianity is carried out with an eye for explicit and accurate knowledge. It appears that his own participation in the broad course of events with which he is concerned was so limited that he might well fail to mention it in his compact preface, and refer specifically only to his own dependence upon the apostolic tradition which was at the foundation of Luke and of a considerable portion of Acts. On this view Luke emphasizes both his dependence and his independence. He is dependent upon tradition, the most competent tradition. But he is not a mere reviser of the efforts of his predecessors. His language is flexible enough, indeed, to allow for a use of the writings of his predecessors, including the Gospel according to Mark, whenever such use might prove helpful. But the principal claim which he makes, and that with considerable force, is that, rather than having been necessarily dependent upon his predecessors, he was in the fortunate position of having been able to undertake a comprehensive and accurate inquiry into the course of Christian history as that had been disclosed to the church by the original witnesses.

In view of the extraordinary importance of these conclusions as to Luke's meaning we shall not dismiss this point without examining a quite different evaluation. Henry J. Cadbury, whose considerations of the meaning of the prologue are among the most learned and stimulating of modern studies devoted to it, maintains that Luke is here claiming that he was actually present at and participated in the events as a member of the group of eye-witness-ministers. To this judgment, moreover, is joined the radical charge that the claim to belong to the category of eye-witnesses must be understood as largely rhetorical and conventional.[2] Appealing to prefaces in historical writings of that era,

[1] See Creed's comments. It is of interest that Cadbury appears to allow for this interpretation in *Beginnings*, I, ii, p. 501 (2), although, as will be observed below, his own viewpoint is quite different.

[2] *Making of Luke-Acts*, pp. 346 f.: 'Thus παρηκολουθηκότι claims something better than research, namely, first-hand or contemporary knowledge and ἄνωθεν carries back, not from the ministry of John to Luke's birth stories, but from the time of writing back over a considerable period of the author's

and concluding that Luke's preface is typical, Cadbury infers that the claim of intimate association with the facts must be largely discounted. On this view Luke is made to claim to be an eyewitness in a very comprehensive way—although he has usually been thought to distinguish carefully between himself and the eyewitnesses. And he is thought to be giving convincing proof that his claims are largely formal—although most readers have gained the impression that he was in dead earnest in establishing his qualifications to provide *certainty* regarding the matters in which Theophilus, and doubtless countless others, had been instructed. Cadbury's interpretation is accordingly nothing short of revolutionary. But nothing is achieved by dismissing the revolutionary with a shrug of the shoulders. In view of the far-reaching implications and standing of this interpretation, we shall do well to give it serious consideration.

First of all, we must examine the interpretation of the language which Cadbury translates 'since I have been now for a long time back in immediate touch with everything circumstantially.'[1] Though Cadbury has a point in protesting against certain modernizing interpretations which apparently conceive of Luke as engaging in research after a modern manner, we cannot agree that he does justice to what Luke actually says.

At least three exegetical considerations militate against Cadbury's interpretation. The first of these is that Luke too sharply distinguishes himself from the group of eyewitness-ministers and too clearly allies himself with the many predecessors, to allow for this interpretation. This appears pointedly in Luke's declaration that 'it seemed good *to me also* to write.'[2]

own association with the movement he is describing.' In *Beginnings*, I, ii, pp. 501 ff., he allows for various other possibilities. He seems, moreover, to acknowledge the difficulty, on his own interpretation of 'follow' as signifying actual presence at the events, of construing the adverb ἀκριβῶς with the participle. He judges that this difficulty may be overcome by taking the adverb with the infinitive 'to write' (p. 504). J. H. Ropes, *The Synoptic Gospels*, p. 62, agrees with the view preferred by Cadbury, and translates: 'since I have been closely and competently associated with everything for a long time back.'

[1] *Making*, p. 347. The RSV rendering, 'having followed all things closely (mg. accurately) for some time past,' apparently reflects this exegesis.

[2] Cadbury himself virtually supports this argument when he says that 'the καί in κἀμοί classes the "me," referring to the author, with the πολλοί who had made attempts to construct a narrative, not with the givers of the tradition'

Sceondly, this construction apparently requires the weakening of ἄνωθεν—'from the beginning'—to 'for a long time back.' On this view, Luke does not have in mind the familiarity which he had acquired with all things from the beginning, including the birth narratives and the baptism of Jesus, but is speaking only generally of his own association with the movement he is describing from the time of his writing *back over a considerable period*. The 'we'-sections of Acts indicate, in truth, that Luke was actually present when some of the events he records took place, but these sections comprehend only small, and rather late, portions of his narrative. And even if one might stretch his personal contact to embrace a somewhat broader period, he would still have to be denied any personal contact with the momentous developments recorded in Luke and in the beginnings of the Acts. Since Luke's purpose is to provide Theophilus with certainty as to the things concerning which he has been informed, and to write broadly concerning 'the things fulfilled among us,' he can hardly be supposed to be content to indicate as his qualification for this comprehensive task the fact that, for hardly more than the last quarter of the period covered, he himself had been in touch with the course of events. Theophilus could not be expected to be assured to any great extent on the basis of such a meagre claim. If Luke is to be understood as engaging in more than mere formalities, he must be commending to his readers his entire work, including especially his account of the earlier events which were not so easily capable of confirmation to persons remote from the time and place of their occurrence as the later happenings.

Finally, the adverb 'accurately' receives scant emphasis on this view, or none at all. In his earlier study Cadbury construes the adverb with the infinitive 'to write' rather than with the participle 'having followed,' and thereby cuts the Gordian knot of the difficulty. In the later study, however, while not indicating his grounds for making the change, he definitely takes the adverb as a qualification of the participle. It seems clear that the rhythm and balance of the sentence are decisive for the latter view which

(p. 510), but he apparently fails to take this into account in his final estimate of Luke's meaning, at least not as formulated in his later treatise, *The Making of Luke-Acts*.

takes the adverb with 'having followed.'[1] But how can the adverb be construed with 'having followed' if the latter means merely 'having been in immediate touch through my presence and participation in the events?' Cadbury seeks to meet this difficulty by translating the adverb 'circumstantially.'[2] However, such an adverb would not so much qualify his association with the course of events as his qualification to write because of his contacts. Cadbury, in commenting on the meaning of the adverb, insists that it refers to 'explicitness of information.'[3] He fails, however, to observe that explicitness of information could be only *the result* of participation in certain events, and that it could hardly characterize participation in them. In other words, if due weight is given to this adverb, it transports us from the sphere of mere association in certain events to that of evaluation and critical judgment with regard to them.

Lest the impression be given that Cadbury bases his view of the thrust of the prologue solely on his exegesis of the participial clause which has been under consideration, we shall give some attention here to another exegetical argument. This argument relates to the reference in the second verse, which has been considered above, to 'those who from the beginning were eyewitnesses and ministers of the word.' On the basis of his examination of its diction and grammar, Cadbury is prepared to indicate his basic agreement with this rendering.[4] His own particular interpretation, however, finds more precise expression in the translation, 'those who had been at the start witnesses and helpers in the mission.'[5] The rendering 'helpers in the mission,' as a substitute for the more familiar 'ministers of the word,' reflects one of the chief reasons advanced in support of Cadbury's thesis. This rendering is based upon the observation that the Greek word ὑπηρέτης translated as 'ministers' or 'helpers' is employed in Acts xiii. 5 with reference to Mark as one who accompanied Barnabas and Paul on their missionary journey. Since the activity of the two leaders is described as proclamation of *the*

[1] Creed, ad loc. Cf. Blass, op. cit., p. 10.

[2] Or 'minutely,' 'particularly,' 'carefully' (*Making*, p. 347; *Beginnings*, I, ii, p. 504. Ropes, op. cit., p. 62, translates it by 'competently.'

[3] *Making*, p. 346.

[4] *Beginnings*, I, ii, p. 498.

[5] *Making*, p. 347.

word (Acts xiii. 5, cf. xv. 36), it is thought that Mark's service must be in that sphere, that Mark is virtually spoken of as a minister of the word (ὑπηρέτης) in Acts xiii. 5, and hence that this reference to Mark recalls the very term used more broadly in the prologue. If, therefore, Mark is specifically in view as one of the 'ministers of the word' or 'helpers in the mission,' Luke himself would similarly qualify, and he would be claiming activity as an eyewitness at this point as well as when he speaks of 'having followed all things from the beginning.'

The appeal of Cadbury to the usage of Acts xiii. 5 as establishing the meaning of Luke in Lk. i. 2 has a degree of plausibility. But a closer examination of the language in the different contexts will disclose that the meaning in Acts xiii. 5 is by no means to be identified with that in Lk. i. 2. The statement in Acts does not describe Mark as a 'minister of the word' but only as a 'helper,' or 'assistant' or 'servant' of Barnabas and Paul. His role was clearly a subordinate one, and the exact service which Mark rendered is not indicated. In the prologue, however, no such subordination is in view, and the translation required in Acts xiii. 5 is not appropriate; the persons referred to are evidently those pre-eminent persons who were the original eyewitnesses and first preachers. A much closer parallel to the usage in the prologue is accordingly found in Acts xxvi. 16 where Paul is referred to as appointed 'a minister and witness both of the things wherein thou hast seen me, and of the things wherein I will appear unto thee.'[1]

Cadbury mentions a third consideration as supporting his conclusion that Luke intends to include himself among the eyewitnesses. His argument is that the 'us' in the phrase 'fulfilled among us' (i. 1) 'cannot possibly exclude eyewitnesses and so we cannot insist upon such an exclusion' in the second use of 'us' in verse 2 where Luke is thought to be referring to his predecessors and himself. With regard to this argument it is sufficient to remark: (1) The word 'us' in verse 1, and perhaps even in verse 2, may have in view the Christian community in general[2] and thus

[1] One may also compare 1 Cor. iv. 1: 'let a man so account of us as of ministers of Christ' (ὑπηρέται Χριστοῦ), although of course 'the word' in Luke i. 2 does not have in mind Christ as the Logos, but the message as in Acts vi. 4.

[2] So Blass, op. cit., p. 14.

would not necessarily include Luke. (2) Even though Luke implies the presence of eyewitnesses among whom the events took place, it is a quite different matter to infer that Luke means to make a direct claim that he is an eyewitness and especially to maintain that such a claim constitutes the main thrust of the prologue.

We conclude, therefore, that the arguments of Professor Cadbury in support of his view that Luke is claiming in the prologue to be an eyewitness who has participated in the events for a long time back are not of sufficient weight to set aside the solid considerations which have been presented to show that Luke carefully distinguishes himself and his predecessors from the company of original eyewitnesses and ministers of the word.

There remains, however, the radical judgment that the claim of Luke to qualify as an eyewitness is shown, by comparison with claims made by other ancient historians, to be merely or largely conventional. Thus it is to be regarded as more rhetorical than factual. This charge has been subjected to a painstaking analysis by F. H. Colson in an article published twenty-five years ago which remains to be answered.[1] After indicating that Cadbury's evidence for the conclusion that the claim to be an eyewitness had become a rhetorical commonplace among historians is not adequately established, and disputing the propriety of speaking of such a practice in general as conventional, as a 'rhetorical commonplace' or 'a literary artifice,' even in those cases where the claims to be an eyewitness and to special knowledge can be shown to be fallacious, Colson declares:

> 'But I fail to see what purpose a "conventional" claim to eyewitnessship in what purports to be sober history can serve. If it ceases to insure credence, it has no *raison d'être*. If I am told that it had no purpose—that writer after writer inserted it because it was the fashion, as we begin letters by "Dear"—then I think it is an unsupported libel on both the seriousness and the literary ability of the age.
>
> 'The utmost then that we can say is that a training in

[1] 'Notes on St. Luke's Preface' in JThS, XXIV, 1923, pp. 300–09. Cf. Creed, p. 4, who says that 'an ancient writer would no more claim the authority of eyewitness without expecting his statement to be believed than a modern.'

rhetoric and a study and observation of historical practice may have contributed to move Luke to put in the forefront of his narrative a statement as to his sources of knowledge, and his claim must be judged on its merits. If that claim is that he himself was an eyewitness of the events in the Gospel, it is manifestly false and he has bungled to boot. For he has managed to give the vast majority of his readers the impression that he does *not* assert eyewitnessship. If the claim is, as we have generally understood, that he had been in touch with the *autoptai* (eyewitnesses) and had carefully observed what they said, then it must be judged by what we conclude otherwise as to his date, accuracy and sincerity. And it is not a whit affected for *better* or worse by the *fact* that he lived in a "rhetorical" age, an age, that is, in which the "ars bene dicendi" was the staple of education, and was more highly valued by the general public than it has been in subsequent times.'[1]

Finally, consideration must be given to Luke's characterization of his own literary activity. The emphasis falls upon the climactic purpose clause which informs us concerning his goal, and we shall be mainly occupied with that subject. The fact may not be overlooked, however, that he mentions as a distinguishing quality of his writing that it was 'in order.'[2]

It has been insisted upon rather widely that Luke must have *chronological* order in mind, and on this understanding he is often thought to be advancing the claim that he is improving upon the chronological order in which the others, including Mark, had presented their materials.[3] That Luke is referring to chronological sequence, is, however, by no means established. As Cadbury points out, this adverb 'does not imply concordance between the order of events and the order of their narration. It means rather a

[1] Pp. 308 f. Cf. Dibelius, op. cit., p. 31.

[2] One should not exaggerate the significance of this characterization as if it were intended by Luke to mark the most distinctive feature of his work, for obviously all that he has to say concerning its contents, his regard for his sources of information, his ability to undertake an inquiry that is both comprehensive and accurate, and his goal in writing—all these affect the decision as to the distinctiveness of Luke's production.

[3] Cf. Meyer (Eng. Trans.), Easton and Creed ad loc.; K. L. Schmidt, *Der Rahmen der Geschichte Jesu*, 1919, p. 317; Jülicher, *Einleitung in das N.T.*, 7th edit., p. 313.

narrative orderly and continuous in itself.'[1] The question of Luke's interest in chronological order, or lack of it, is therefore not determined in advance in his preface. It will have to be decided by evaluation of the data of the narratives which themselves elucidate this point. If I may anticipate here conclusions reached in my study of the Gospel as a whole, the judgment on the present issue may be clarified by the observation that Luke decidedly does not, as compared, for example, with Mark, manifest a special interest in the exact chronological sequence of the separate events. His narratives contain some precise chronological data, and display, of course, a consciousness of the general sequence of events in Luke and Acts, but quite different is the supposition that he aimed to set the several incidents in a precise chronological framework.

The use of the adverb 'in order' (καθεξῆς) is probably, therefore, to be explained as due to Luke's interest in a connected narrative. As distinguished from the narratives of his predecessors, which perhaps were confined to certain phases of the public ministry of Christ, and which for the most part probably were rather abrupt and piece-meal in character, Luke apparently wishes to construct a connected and orderly narrative. Taken with the reference to his interest in 'all things,' he suggests that he wishes to produce a continuous and comprehensive account. That he fulfilled this aim is borne out fully by his achievement in the composition of Luke-Acts which excels in orderliness as in comprehensiveness.

The goal which Luke sets before him is of far-reaching significance for our understanding of his work. Addressing his treatise to 'most excellent Theophilus,' he states as his aim 'that thou mightest know the certainty concerning the matters wherein thou wast instructed.' Nothing more is known concerning him than appears in Luke's allusions here and at the beginning of Acts, but that Theophilus was a real individual, rather than merely a symbolic name for the Christian readers, as 'lovers of God,' is admitted on all sides today. Confirmation of this conclusion is

[1] *Making*, p. 345. Cf. *Beginnings*, I, ii, pp. 504 f., where he suggests 'successively' and 'continuously,' and adds, 'It need not therefore imply accordance with some fixed order, either chronological, geographical, or literary.' See also Klostermann, HB, ad loc., who says that it refers less to chronological accuracy than to 'wohldurchdachte Anordnung'; Blass, p. 18; Greijdanus ad loc.

found especially in the use of the honorific adjective, which Luke later also uses with reference to the procurators Felix and Festus (Acts xxiii. 26, xxiv. 3, xxvi. 25). The epithet is roughly the equivalent of 'your excellency,' and is thus so flexible that one cannot derive from it exact information regarding the rank of Theophilus. That he was a person of some eminence, however, can hardly be doubted.[1]

The question whether or not Theophilus was a Christian when Luke addressed him is of more practical consequence. Since Luke seems clearly to use the designation as a recognition of official rank, we may dismiss the view that Luke would certainly have addressed him as a 'brother' if he had been a Christian at the time.[2] For the same reason we cannot agree with Zahn that the absence of the epithet in Acts i. 1, is evidence that Theophilus had become converted in the interval before Luke undertook the second volume. The issue whether Theophilus was a Christian will have to be determined by other considerations.

Cadbury is the leading advocate of the view that Theophilus was not a Christian but an influential non-Christian, and that, accordingly, the preface contains the implication that Luke-Acts was conceived of as an *apologia* for Christianity. He says, 'We cannot be sure that Theophilus would be more interested in "all that Jesus began both to do and teach" than the second-century emperors were in the works dedicated to them on the Greek word accent (twenty volumes by Herodian), on military strategy (by Aelian and Polyaenus) . . . and many defences of Christianity by the apologists . . .'[3] We may well agree that the address to Theophilus does not carry with it the implication that the work was not intended ultimately for a wide-reading public. Still, the issue remains whether the preface, when studied in relation to the contents of Luke-Acts, allows for the isolation from the Christian movement presupposed by Cadbury's construction. Does it not imply that Theophilus had come into intimate contact with the Christian movement, and had even received

[1] Streeter's speculation that Theophilus may have been a prudential pseudonym for some Roman of position, perhaps Flavius Clemens, cousin of Domitian, is of interest in this connection. Op. cit., pp. 534 ff.

[2] This view is taken by Zahn, *Einleitung*, p. 365; J. Weiss, SNT, I, p. 395; W. Manson, MNT, pp. 2 f.

[3] *Making*, pp. 203 f.

instruction, if not as a confessing Christian or a catechumen, then clearly at least as an inquirer?

The chief exegetical argument relied upon by Cadbury to support his view is drawn from his judgment as to the meaning of the words which have been translated, 'that thou mightest know the certainty concerning the matter wherein thou wast instructed.' If Theophilus received 'instruction' concerning Christianity, that would seem to settle the matter against Cadbury. It must be admitted, however, that the verb translated 'thou wast instructed' does not necessarily presuppose a docile attitude on the part of the person addressed. As the usage in Acts xxi. 21 and 24 indicates, the verb could also be employed where hostile reports are concerned. The verb itself does not determine the issue; it might be used, depending on the context, of the impartation of reports which were either hostile or favourable or quite neutral. Now Cadbury himself does not argue from the use of this verb as such, as is intimated by his suggested rendering: 'that you may gather the correctness as regards the accounts that you have been given to understand.'[1] Although then Cadbury allows a neutral interpretation of the clause in question to stand, he nevertheless argues that the work was nominally 'dedicated or addressed with the intention of meeting incriminating reports or impressions by the presentation of exonerating facts.' The basis for this far-reaching conclusion is formulated in the statement that 'similar passages in Acts deal with the accusation of Christians due to misrepresentations or ignorance, and make it likely that here also they have an apologetic connotation.'[2] The passages in view here are Acts xxi. 34, xxii. 30, and xxv. 26, where there is mention of inquiries as to 'the certainty' (τὸ ἀσφαλές) in connection with certain charges. Do the passages in Acts, however, present true parallels to the statement in Lk. i. 4? In our judgment the pertinent contexts indicate that the parallelism, such as it is, does not affect the substance of the matter.[3]

The situations in Acts have in mind inquiries as to what could be relied upon as to the *nature* of certain charges, not what could be relied upon in the determination of the *truth* of these charges.

[1] *Making*, p. 347; cf. *Beginnings*, I, ii, pp. 509 f.
[2] *Beginnings*, p. 510.
[3] For what follows cf. especially Colson, op. cit., pp 300 ff.

The chief captain who held Paul in chains could not know the certainty as to 'who he was and what he had done,' the reason being that there was an 'uproar' (xxi. 33 f.); there is nothing to suggest that a point had been reached where *the truth* of the charges was to be determined. Later the chief captain made another effort, again apparently without much success, 'to know the certainty whereof he was accused of the Jews' (xxii. 30, cf. xxiii. 1 ff.). Likewise, Festus, possessing 'no certain thing to write' to the emperor, decided upon a hearing in order that 'the charges' against Paul might be signified (xxv. 26 f.).

There is nothing parallel to these situations in Lk. i. 4. The evangelist is clearly not writing to inform Theophilus as to what could be relied upon as to certain charges made against Christianity. Luke intimates nothing as to charges made. He is completely silent concerning incriminating reports. But how could he remain silent on this point if the inquiries in the latter chapters of Acts form genuine parallels to his thought in the prologue? And the apologetic motif of Luke-Acts is not explicit enough to colour Luke's language at this point. What he claims as his goal is to provide Theophilus, who is already an *informed* person, with *certainty* as to the origins of Christianity. Neither the language of the preface nor the disposition of the Lucan narrative, therefore, afford any positive support of the conclusion that the writer has distinctly in view certain incriminating reports which have reached the non-Christian world and that his book has been written to answer these reports. The emphasis upon *thorough* (ἐπιγνῷς) knowledge, and especially upon *certain* knowledge accords rather with the view that Luke had in mind an audience which was favourably informed concerning Christianity, howbeit perhaps in fragmentary and unsystematic fashion, and that what was required was a completely trustworthy record of all things from the beginning in order that faith might be further informed and might receive confirmation.

What, then, is the main impact made by the prologue? It gives explicit expression to the conviction, which obviously all the writers of the New Testament share, that Christianity is true and is capable of confirmation by appeal to what had happened. Christianity according to Luke was no mere ideology, nor a pragmatic or positivist philosophy of life or ethic. For him it stood or fell with the objective reality of certain happenings, which took place in the full light of day, in the midst of a considerable company who made up the membership of the Christian church, were reported by competent witnesses, and had become widely known.

For himself Luke claims the competence to provide a completely trustworthy account of what had happened, so that he could satisfy the need of any who lacked assurance. He does not make any explicit claim to be an organ of divine inspiration. He does not say that 'it seemed good to the Holy Spirit and to me to write.'[1] Nevertheless, the confidence with which Luke assures his readers of the truth of his record is profoundly congruous, to say the least, with the fact of divine inspiration. The consideration that the council at Jerusalem invoked the authority of the Holy Spirit in its formal decree would not require on Luke's part an express avowal of inspiration as the basis of his completely trustworthy narrative. Only if divine inspiration had to operate in a mechanical fashion, quite apart from historical inquiry and with indifference to personal qualities, would there be a contradiction between Luke's claims and the implications of canonicity.[2] Luke says nothing directly about inspiration but the fact remains that his claim that he is publishing a completely reliable narrative poses a most serious problem for those who deny his trustworthiness. To some students of Luke he must indeed appear exceedingly presumptuous or self-deceived. But to others his claims are received as uttered in all soberness and his work continues to be read with a view to the attainment of certainty regarding the things that Jesus did and taught among men.

[1] Cf. Jülicher, op. cit., p. 459, and Acts xv. 28. Note, however, that Klostermann says that the expression 'it seems to me' does not as such exclude inspiration, although in certain MSS. of the Old Latin it is joined by the phrase 'et spiritu sancto.'

[2] Inspiration may be a fact even where there is no specific claim, for in receiving the Old Testament as divine Scripture the Lord acknowledged as canonical several books which make no direct claims of inspiration. In the case of the apostolic decree, Luke felt no incongruity in accepting the decree as given by the Holy Spirit and the fact that it was formulated on the background of discussion at the council.

CHAPTER III

THE GOSPEL AND THE HISTORICAL BEGINNINGS

AMONG the things 'fulfilled among us,' concerning which Luke writes with the purpose of establishing and confirming Christian faith, first place is given to the beginnings of the life of Jesus Christ. In this respect his approach to the publication of the gospel is at one with Matthew's. Whereas Mark is content to intimate the presence in the world of the Son of God, and John rather abruptly affirms that the eternal Logos 'became flesh and dwelt among us,' Matthew and Luke report at length concerning the circumstances of His birth. The very agreement with Matthew, however, serves to centre attention upon the distinctiveness of the Lucan account. If Luke's narrative merely supplemented at some length what Matthew had set forth with comparative brevity, our problem would be relatively simple. But the fact is that the considerably greater extent of Luke's account is not its most basic difference. Indeed, Luke's narrative appears hardly to coincide with Matthew's at all. Little wonder that the diversity of the two reports of the birth of Jesus should have led in modern times to questions as to the historicity of one or the other. Our concern here is not with questions of historicity, but rather with interpretation. But the diversity of Luke and Matthew do challenge the interpreter to gauge aright the disposition of Luke in relation to that of Matthew, and to take some account of the problems raised by their divergences.

Matthew confines his narrative basically to a brief description of the virgin birth of Jesus Christ. In addition he shows how Joseph came to wed Mary in spite of his discovery of her condition, and explains, by reference to prophecy, how God safeguarded the life of the newborn son of David in the face of the violent efforts of the reigning king of the Jews to destroy Him. Since this account tells of private experiences which Joseph or Mary alone could have reported, the tradition apparently goes back to them. Nevertheless, only so much of the private life of the family is told as explains the course of events which were more or less of a public nature, namely, the marriage of Joseph and Mary and the flight into Egypt.

In contrast Luke sets forth many minute details of the life of the family into which Jesus was born. The intimate disclosures that Mary would have given only to her closest confidants are set down. As one follows Mary through various stages of her extraordinary experience, her very soul seems to be laid bare. It is this intimate, revealing nature of Luke's narration, together with features like the glowing prophetic poetry of Mary and Zacharias, which accounts chiefly for the irresistible charm of these chapters.

Another distinguishing feature of the Lucan narrative is the place given to the birth of John the Baptist. His birth is solemnly announced (Lk. i. 5-25) and later its occurrence and the extraordinary attendant circumstances are related at length (Lk. i. 57-80). The parallelism of these sections with those which tell of the announcement of the birth of Jesus and of his birth itself (Lk. i. 25-38, ii. 1-7) gives added prominence to the history of the Baptist.

One might judge from these features of the Lucan narrative that the writing is distinguished from Matthew's because of the biographical interest of its author. Thus the intimate details of the life of the family of Jesus, including the psychological observations concerning Mary, might be explained. The attention given to the Baptist might also be accounted for as due to a biographer's or historian's interest to satisfy curiosity as to the origins of the leading personalities in the Christian movement. Such conclusions appear, however, not to be well founded in fact, as I shall show at length in the discussion in this chapter.

REVELATION AND HISTORY

The actual disposition of Luke is recognized only when it is observed that the intimate details concerning Mary and the Baptist and the other secondary figures of the story are set forth only because they illumine the significance of the birth of Christ, and so contribute to the proclamation of the gospel. In particular these historical details provide the occasions for a long series of inspired disclosures which cast a brilliant light upon the Child who was born in Bethlehem. There is, therefore, no disparagement of history. Luke clearly intends to provide a record of a series of actual happenings. His narrative is a record of events, and especially of one great event. That momentous event, around which everything else turns and to which everything else points, is the fact that Jesus was born of the virgin Mary in the town of Bethlehem.[1] That event is set forth as a divine act. But if no further explanation were offered, it would be quite unintelligible. The cluster of divine revelation, which both precedes and follows the account of the birth of Jesus, serves, however, to expound the true significance of the divine action.

Matthew also views the birth of Christ in terms of divine revelation. But he sees the history of Christ mainly as the fulfilment of the prophecy of the Old Testament, a fulfilment that comes to realization only because of the divine government of events as God guides and protects the course of events to their appointed end. This element is not completely lacking in Luke. He tells of the annunciation of the Son of David who fulfils the promise that He should reign over the house of Jacob for ever, and recalls the assurance that of His kingdom there should be no end (Lk. i. 32 f., cf. v. 69). But in the main the revelational message reported by Luke is a *contemporary* prophetic message, which, though breathing the atmosphere of Old Testament prophecy, points to the imminent manifestation of the divine presence and power through the birth of the son of Mary. This contemporary annunciation of the coming One is itself a preaching of glad tidings (Lk. i. 19, ii. 10),[2] and thus, in spite of its prophetic mould, it is a constituent element of the gospel of Jesus Christ to which Luke bears witness. The gospel, according to Luke, is therefore divine not merely as a word of prophecy spoken through the prophets; nor again merely because that prophecy has been fulfilled by divine action, but also because the present divine action is accompanied by inspired utterances. As this conclusion is supported in detail, it will appear how far removed Luke is from approaching his subject as a modern

[1] It should not be overlooked that, in spite of the diversity of the birth narratives of Matthew and Luke, Matthew also sets forth this central fact (cf. Mt. ii. 1). He also reports that after some time Mary and Joseph took up residence in Nazareth (Mt. ii. 1, 23; cf. Lk. ii. 1 ff., 39, iv. 16).

[2] εὐαγγελίζομαι is used both in the announcement of Gabriel to Zacharias and in the message of the angel to the shepherds.

biographer. He writes as a publisher of the glad tidings of Jesus Christ.

The extent to which Luke is occupied with contemporaneous revelation will appear most graphically from the following outline of the narrative of events and the accompanying disclosures:

1. Announcement of the birth of John (Lk. i. 5-25).
   (*a*) Disclosure of the Angel of the Lord concerning John's mission to go before the Lord in the spirit and power of Elijah (i. 7, cf. i. 13-17, 19-20).
2. Announcement of the birth of Jesus (i. 26-38).
   (*b*) Communications of the Angel Gabriel to Mary: she shall conceive a son through the overshadowing of the power of the Most High, a son who shall be called the Son of God and who shall reign over the house of Jacob forever (i. 28, 30-33, 35).
3. Visit of Mary to Elizabeth (i. 39-56).
   (*c*) Elizabeth, 'full of the Holy Spirit,' addresses Mary as 'the mother of my Lord' (i. 43, cf. verses 42-45).
   (*d*) Mary's response: she magnifies the Lord for His mercy in fulfilment of His covenant (i. 46-55).
4. The birth of John (i. 57-79; cf. verse 80).
   (*e*) Zacharias prophesies, blessing the God of Israel because He had visited and wrought redemption for His people, and declaring that John should be called the prophet of the Most High, who would go before the face of the Lord to make ready His ways.
5. The birth of Jesus (ii. 1-7).
6. Visit of the shepherds (ii. 8-20).
   (*f*) Proclamation of the angel of the good tidings of a Saviour, who is Christ the Lord (ii. 10-12).
   (*g*) Song of the heavenly hosts ascribing glory to God and proclaiming the message of peace to those who are the objects of the divine good-pleasure (ii. 14).
7. Circumcision of Jesus and giving of name Jesus in accordance with angelic disclosure (ii. 21).
8. Presentation at Jerusalem (ii. 22-38).
   (*h*) Oracle to Simeon by the Holy Spirit that he would not die before he should see the Lord's Christ (ii. 26).

(*i*) Simeon's prophecy concerning the manifestation of salvation, a salvation for Gentiles as well as Israel, and his word to Mary that the coming of her Son will result in the fall as well as the rising of many in Israel (ii. 29, 34, 35).

(*j*) Anna, a prophetess, spoke of Him to all them that were looking for the redemption of Jerusalem (ii. 38).

9. Return to Nazareth (ii. 39, 40).
10. Visit of the boy Jesus to Jerusalem (ii. 41-52).

(*k*) Jesus's declaration that He must be about His Father's concerns (ii. 49).

These eleven disclosures, accordingly, are not merely incidental to the story of the birth of Jesus. They are not presented simply to dress up the narrative in a poetic manner. Rather they are of the very warp and woof of Luke's message concerning Jesus. Through angelic annunciations and prophetic communications, and finally (in a somewhat detached manner), through the intimation of Jesus Himself, we observe the true significance of the event upon which Luke concentrates our attention. The disclosures, like the birth of Jesus itself, are distinctly supernatural, and both the nature of His birth and the revelations accompanying it point to the supernatural person presented to men in the gospel.

The witness of the birth narratives to the person of Christ is remarkable for the manner in which various strands of the Biblical revelation converge within it to bring before the reader a most illuminating and even overwhelming portrayal of the divine Messiah. The one who is born is named Jesus (i. 31, ii. 21), who is the Christ, the Lord's Anointed (ii. 26). As Messiah He is the Son of David, who will occupy eternally the throne of His father David and reign over the house of Jacob for ever (i. 32 f.). As the One who is begotten through the coming of the Holy Spirit and the overshadowing of the Most High, He is appropriately called Son of God (i. 35). But His coming is also viewed as being nothing less than the long-awaited coming of the Lord Himself (i. 17, 76; cf. i. 43, ii. 11), so that we are confronted with the staggering paradox that He who is the Lord's Anointed (*Christos Kyriou*) is in truth the Lord Himself (*Christos Kyrios*). His place and mission in the history of revelation and redemption receive further clarification when His coming is viewed as accomplishing the fulfilment of the covenant established with Abraham (i. 54 f., 72 f.) and as effecting the redemption and salvation of Israel (i. 68, ii. 38, i. 69, 77, ii. 11,30; cf. i. 47).

THE ROLE OF SIMEON

These summary observations as to the disposition of the Lucan birth narrative may be set in sharper relief when the details of certain episodes are subjected to closer scrutiny. The record of Simeon's utterances concerning Christ affords a particularly illuminating example of Luke's perspective. And the consideration of Simeon's role will prove especially instructive when compared with the place occupied by the career and testimony of the Baptist.

As compared with the Baptist, Simeon played a distinctly secondary part. He did not attract the notice of his contemporaries; he was merely 'a man in Jerusalem' (ii. 25). His significance is seen to be exhausted in his appraisal of Christ. But that appraisal is noteworthy because of Simeon's personal and historical qualifications as a pious Israelite, a prophet to whom was disclosed the nearness of the coming of the Messiah, and a witness of the fulfilment of that revelation.

In the first place, he was 'righteous and devout,' a man distinguished for godliness of life and by godly fear in a time of lawlessness and apostasy. And his piety is seen to be no mere mysticism, but to be rooted in the Biblical historical revelation in that he was 'looking for the consolation of Israel.' The consolation of Israel was nothing other than the messianic hope of which the prophets had spoken. Isaiah especially characterized the coming age as one of consolation or comfort for the people of God:

> 'Comfort ye, comfort ye my people, saith your God.
> Speak ye comfortably to Jerusalem,
> And cry unto her, that her warfare is accomplished,
> That her iniquity is pardoned.'
>
> (Is. xl. 1, 2; cf. xlix. 13; li. 3)

Among the duties of the Anointed of the Lord, as described in Is. lxi, there is the charge

'To comfort all that mourn;
To appoint unto them that mourn in Zion,
To give unto them a garland for ashes,
The oil of joy for mourning,
The garment of praise for the spirit of heaviness;
That they may be called trees of righteousness,
The planting of the Lord, that He might be glorified.'

(lxi. 2, 3.)

Laden with iniquity, afflicted and oppressed, the people of God is offered the happy prospect of a new day when the grace and power of the Lord of Hosts will have accomplished her salvation. Simeon as a true child of God enjoyed the God-centred faith which rested in the divine promise and found its expectation in God. His religion, the revealed and enjoined religion of the Scriptures, was accordingly eschatological.

But Simeon was more than a pious man; he was a prophet. As one who was called to speak on God's behalf to men he was granted a direct and special revelation of the divine purpose. A solemn oracular utterance came to him through the Holy Spirit, and the extraordinary content of this disclosure was that before he should die he would see the Lord's Christ (ii. 26)! The consolation of Israel was to be accomplished through the coming of the Anointed of the Lord, the Messiah commissioned and endowed by the living, covenant God. So much was what the prophets had repeatedly declared. But the new ingredient was that the fulfilment of the messianic expectation was so near at hand that the waiting was virtually over. The ends of the ages have come. The greatest event in history is about to be unfolded, and Simeon is immediately at hand.

The divine word of prophecy is now fulfilled through Simeon's encounter with the child Jesus (ii. 27 f.). Mary and Joseph, having come to Jerusalem to fulfil the law regarding purification in the case of the birth of a firstborn son, actually prepared the way for the fulfilment of messianic prophecy in general and particularly the contemporaneous prophecy to Simeon. What many prophets and righteous men had desired to see, but did not, Simeon was now given the privilege of seeing (cf. Mt. xiii. 17). But not content with merely beholding the Messiah, he embraced

Him, thus expressing his fervour and enthusiasm at what had overtaken him. All centred then in the great fact of the coming of Christ, an event for which the divine prophecy had been preparing men in order that, when it took place, it might be understood at its true worth. The presence of this babe in Simeon's arms, seemingly quite like countless other instances of tender regard shown to infants in the history of the race, was thus viewed as an absolutely unique historical phenomenon. The Lord Himself is present in His Anointed One to accomplish the redemption of His people.

There now follow the moving words of Simeon's Song, the *Nunc Dimittis*, filling out the preparatory revelation with further reflection upon the historic significance of what had taken place. 'Now, O Sovereign Master, Thou art releasing Thy slave in peace for mine eyes have seen Thy salvation' (ii. 29, 30). Salvation has come in the person of this child; the consolation of Israel is realized. This is the gospel of salvation in the one name given under heaven among men by which we must be saved (cf. iii. 6, i. 69, 71, 79; Acts iv. 12, xxviii. 28). The peculiar personal reaction of Simeon serves only to make more vivid the sense of the decisiveness of what has taken place. The language employed serves to describe the release from service of a servant, or more probably the manumission of a slave, with death regarded as the liberating agent which is used by the sovereign master. In the context it appears, moreover, that the special task of the slave is that of a watchman. Accordingly, Simeon's words give powerful expression to the thought that Simeon, having beheld Christ in fulfilment of the divine word concerning his life, has fully performed his service. His watch is concluded with the arrival of the One for whom he was waiting. The watchman may now retire; the slave may in truth now be emancipated. There is nothing more to do, there is nothing more to live for. And therefore in confidence Simeon addresses his Lord with the words, 'And now, O Sovereign Master, Thou are releasing Thy slave in peace for mine eyes have seen Thy salvation.'

Here, then, we are confronted with the recognition of an event of history as constituting divine action and thus, as also, being an objectively valid revelation. This is not mere historism, not the attaching of religious or revelational value to merely human history. It is not a religion rooted in nothing higher historically than the impression made by the personality of Jesus upon men. It is not an attachment to his message as a timeless idealism which has significance and is valid quite apart from one's thought concerning the truth of the history of Jesus Christ. The very presence in the world of this babe of Bethlehem, well before his public ministry could be discharged in terms of deeds and words, was acknowledged as the manifestation of the divine action of salvation. Bound up as it was with the person of Christ and his appearance in the world, it possessed a finality and exclusiveness, a decisive once-for-all character, that gave the religion based upon it a character of its own, far removed from mystic idealism or similar expressions of religiosity which think to preserve the interests of religion by divorcing it from what are regarded as the contingencies of history.

But in addition to the accent upon *historical* salvation, we encounter certain other evaluations of the significance of the coming of Christ which enlarge our view of Simeon's witness to Christ. That the salvation now in view is *universal* is conspicuously brought to mind. The salvation proclaimed and being realized is that which God 'prepared before the face of all peoples, a light for revelation to the Gentiles and glory for thy people Israel' (Lk. ii. 31 f.). The universality of Christianity, while it awaited historical developments to be grasped in its fuller implications and realized in practice, is thus rooted in the revelation contemporaneous with the birth of Christ. But this revelation in turn is but a reiteration of an arresting feature of the earlier prophetic testimony, in fact the very words employed here echo the language of Isaiah:

'The Lord hath made bare His holy arm
In the eyes of all the nations;
And all the ends of the earth shall see
The salvation of our God.'

(Is. lii. 10.)

'And the glory of the Lord shall be revealed,
And all flesh shall see it together:
For the mouth of the Lord hath spoken it.'

(Is. xl. 5.)

The particularization of this salvation into light for revelation to the Gentiles and glory for Israel also, partially at least, reflects the language of Isaiah concerning the mission of the Servant:

'It is too light a thing that Thou shouldest be my servant
To raise up the tribes of Jacob,
And to restore the preserved of Israel:
I will also give Thee for a light to the Gentiles
That Thou mayest be My salvation unto the end of the earth.'
(xlix. 6; cf. xlii. 6.)

It is not insignificant that Luke, who was to show how the universalism of Christianity came to be realized in the early history of Christianity, underscores here at the beginning the universality of the gospel as a note of the revelation contemporaneous with Christ's birth. But Simeon's prophecy is characterized by the same restraint that marks the prophetic testimonies of these chapters generally. In declaring that the salvation to be realized through the new-born Messiah was to be 'a light for revelation and glory for thy people Israel,' Simeon hardly becomes more specific than the prophets of earlier centuries. Only the historical note that the fulfilment of such prophecy was now in process of actual realization is new.

A somewhat different accent appears in the closing words of Simeon. In the midst of the joyous song of universal salvation a most sombre chord is heard. Though the glory of Israel was about to be realized through her Messiah, the fact had to be recorded that 'this Child is set for the falling . . . of many in Israel; and for a sign which is spoken against' (ii. 34). There comes to expression at this point a thought which was to be expounded profoundly by the apostle Paul in Romans ix–xi, where he declares that according to the divine purpose 'they are not all Israel who are of Israel' (Rom. ix. 6). Jesus Himself, as the passion narratives disclose with special clearness, anticipated His rejection on the part of Israel and also taught that He had come to bring division (Mt. x. 34 ff.). But this feature, as introduced by Simeon in the birth narratives of Luke, is not a novelty. For like the theme of the universality of the gospel it also appears in the prophets. Just as behind the historical universalism of the New Testament there is a deeper particularism bound up with the sovereign operations of God's grace and with the rejection of the gospel on the part of sinful men, so there was already behind the rather pervasive historical particularism of the Old Testament a more basic particularism which constantly stands in judgment upon the presumption of any race or any individual to appear in the presence of Him who alone is holy, apart from the divine redemption and apart from genuine conversion. Among the many expressions of this motif mention may be made here only of the doctrine of the remnant. Again and again the warning is given that only a remnant shall be saved, and that this in itself is a wonder of grace (cf., e.g., Is. i. 9, x. 22 f.). And Isaiah declared also that the Lord Himself would be 'a stone of stumbling and rock of offence to both the houses of Israel' (viii. 14), and that the Servant of the Lord, who would justify many and bear their iniquities, was despised and rejected of man (liii. 3, 11).

Only when Simeon speaks, particularly concerning Mary's own personal experience, of a sword which would pierce through her own soul (ii. 35), does he pass from the rather general prophetic witness to a concrete prediction concerning what was about to take place. But once the fact is recognized that the universality of the promised salvation is bound up with its divisive particularism, the prophecy of Mary's anguish will be seen to be of a piece with Simeon's acknowledgment of the presence of the divine salvation in the person of Jesus. The historical realization of the divine salvation was perceived as being so imminent that the rejection of the Child as the sign appointed by God would spell the sharpest smart for His mother. Here the cross is indeed virtually in view, and Mary is standing before it, sorrowing at what would befall her son. Nevertheless the utmost restraint is employed in tracing beforehand the course of the ministry of the Lord's Anointed who was 'set for the falling and rising of many in Israel.' His manifestation would disclose 'the thoughts of many hearts' as men either embraced Him, as Simeon did, or repudiated the divine revelation which He embodied.

THE MISSION OF THE BAPTIST

While, then, Simeon is introduced and is significant only for the sake of his inspired testimony to Christ, John the Baptist emerges as a figure of considerable historical proportions and importance.

His birth and career are set forth so fully and conspicuously that it might appear that he is presented for his own sake, as a figure alongside of Jesus who contributed substantially to the origins of the Christian movement. While all the Gospels give prominence to John, Luke contains a number of distinctive features which place the role of John in even sharper focus and seem to attest a large measure of independence.

Reference has already been made to the striking parallelism of presentation of the birth of John and that of Jesus: a parallelism commencing with angelic annunciations of their births and extending to the records of their occurrence as fulfilments of the supernatural announcements. Moreover, the birth of John, as well as that of Jesus, is followed by solemn disclosures which provide further authoritative interpretations of what had happened. In the case of John, his father Zacharias, filled with the Holy Spirit, describes his son prophetically as 'prophet of the Most High' (i. 76). That the parallelism extends to other material features as well as to the formal aspects is seen, moreover, from the occupation of the narrative with the extraordinary character of John's birth. Although only the origin of Jesus is set forth as distinctly miraculous, in virtue of the conception by the Holy Spirit and birth of the Virgin, John's birth is shown to have been no ordinary event. Emphasis is laid upon the facts that Elizabeth was barren and that both she and Zacharias were advanced in years, and there are definite intimations that the child was conceived only as the result of an intervention of divine favour. The father was punished with dumbness for a time because of his failure to believe the divine promise communicated by the angel Gabriel, but Elizabeth rejoices in the promise and work of the Lord (i. 17, 18, 20, 25, 45, 58). She acknowledges, 'Thus hath the Lord done unto me in the days wherein He looked upon me, to take away my reproach among men' (i. 25).

Luke's testimony concerning the career of the Baptist also emphasizes the significance of John's ministry. His message is reported more fully than in the other synoptic Gospels. There is also a summary statement of John's 'many other exhortations,' in which his preaching is distinctively characterized as a proclamation of 'good tidings,' as the angelic proclamation had been described previously (iii. 10-14, 18; cf. i. 19, ii. 10). Except for

Matthew's use in xi. 15, Luke alone of the evangelists employs this verb εὐαγγελίζεσθαι to characterize the preaching of Jesus.[1] This is a further example of the way in which the agreement of John's message with that of Jesus is emphasized.

More arresting is the manner in which the public career of the Baptist is introduced. One of the most impressive features of the early chapters of the Gospel is the elaborate synchronism with which Luke marks the beginning of the ministry of John:

> 'Now in the fifteenth year of the reign of Tiberius Caesar, Pontius Pilate being governor of Judæa, and Herod being tetrarch of Galilee, and his brother Philip tetrarch of the region of Ituraea and Trachonitis, and Lysanias tetrarch of Abilene, in the high-priesthood of Annas and Caiaphas, the word of God came unto John the son of Zacharias in the wilderness' (iii. 1, 2).

Some of these secular and religious rulers may have been introduced here because of their participation in the ensuing development. However, as the reference to the fifteenth year of Tiberius particularly shows, foremost in the evangelist's mind must have been the desire to indicate precisely when the movement began in which John was to play a conspicuous part.

Still, even this single indication of time is not completely without ambiguity. Since Augustus, the predecessor of Tiberius, died on the 19th of August A.D. 14, it might appear that the time when 'the word of God came unto John' fell within the year beginning on the 19th of August A.D. 28. Two important considerations, however, affect the decision. In the first place, the common mode of reckoning apparently followed the calendar year rather than the dynastic year, and in all likelihood the Jewish year would have been in Luke's mind. It is therefore more satisfactory in the context of Luke to suppose that the reckoning is from the first of Nisan rather than from the 19th of August. John may then have begun his ministry within the year beginning 1st Nisan A.D. 28, and concluding on the same date A.D. 29.[2]

[1] Cf. Lk. iv. 18, 43, vii. 22, viii. 1, ix. 16, xvi. 16, xx. 1. It is also used fifteen times in Acts of the Christian proclamation of the gospel. On the meaning of 'gospel' see WMMC, pp. 10 ff.

[2] Cf. especially G. Ogg, *The Chronology of the Public Ministry of Jesus*, 1940, pp. 184 ff., and my review in WTJ IV. 1 (Nov. 1941), pp. 38 ff., 42 f.

In the second place, it is quite possible that Luke has in view a time two or three years earlier than A.D. 28, reckoning from the time when Tiberius began to be associated with Augustus. Otherwise Luke's own reference to the approximate age of Jesus at the time of the commencement of his public ministry (iii. 23: 'about thirty years of age') would require us to place the birth of Jesus considerably later than the death of Herod (4 B.C.). This difficulty is removed if the baptism of Jesus occurred considerably before 28 or 29.[1] In spite of difficulties of this character, however, the interest of Luke to indicate the historical setting of the beginnings of the Christian movement in its public phase is plain.

This synchronism, together with a number of somewhat less elaborate historical and chronological data in Luke, have strongly contributed to the judgment that Luke is 'the historian' among the evangelists. He reflects indeed the consciousness that the events he narrates concern a movement which found expression, not in some remote corner of the world, but in the midst of the Roman empire in the full light of day. In his grandly conceived work Luke tells how this movement had its beginnings in the vassal kingdom of Herod, in Judæa (i. 5), in the province of Syria, while Caesar Augustus was emperor (ii. 1 f.). He reflects further how Christianity became a public movement during the reign of Tiberius Caesar, when sons of Herod, as tetrarchs rather than as kings, ruled over the northern regions of Palestine while in Judæa proper a Roman procurator had stepped in the place of another son who had been deposed (iii. 1 f.). And he proceeds to tell how, after the ascension of Christ, His message and church made their way under other Herods and many governors from Jerusalem to Rome, in a world which everywhere recognized the sovereignty of Roman emperors. For Luke, therefore, Christianity was a movement specifically within the framework of world history.

Now the fact that it is John's ministry, rather than Christ's, which Luke introduces with this elaborate and formal synchronism seems to some to offer proof that Luke is controlled by the approach of the secular historian rather than by a pervasively

[1] See W. P. Armstrong, 'Chronology of the New Testament,' in ISBE, I, p. 647; C. H. Turner, 'Chronology of the NT,' in HDB, I, pp. 405 f.; my review of Ogg, WTJ, IV. 1, p. 43.

theological or christological interest as a publisher of the gospel of Jesus Christ. There is something approaching the disconcerting in the special attention bestowed upon John, and it is not surprising that the history of the exegesis of this passage has yielded interpretations to the effect that Luke, as an historian of Christ's life, must have in view some event in the life of our Lord rather than in the life of the Baptist.[1] It is true, indeed, that this formal and elaborate description of the beginning of John's ministry attaches great importance to his role within the foundational history of Christianity. However, this narration of the commencement of John's public mission is not the reader's introduction to John nor does it stand in isolation from what has gone before. Its integration with the testimony to John within the birth narratives appears in sharpest focus from Lk. i. 80, where we read that John 'grew, and waxed strong in spirit, and was in the deserts *till the day of his showing to Israel.*' The reader has been prepared to expect the dawn of a great day when John would come forth from his obscurity to herald the coming of the Christ. Commenting on Lk. i. 80, J. Gresham Machen has said:

> 'Does that verse not lead the reader to look for the great day that is there held in prospect, the day when John would emerge from his obscurity and appear publicly as the forerunner of the messianic salvation? Whenever that day should come, surely it would be heralded by the writer who included i. 80 in his book, with all the solemnity that he could command. And just exactly that is done in Lk. iii. 1 f. The period of obscurity and waiting in which the reader was left in the former passage is over; the forerunner emerges from the deserts and the day of the messianic salvation has dawned. What wonder that the concomitant political conditions are marked with all the precision that the writer can command; what wonder that rulers and high priests are marshalled to do honour to the great event that signalized their reign?'[2]

[1] Cf. Ogg, op. cit., p. 192, for a survey of such opinions: Caspari refers it to the baptism of Christ; Wieseler to the Galilean ministry; Loisy and Goguel to the crucifixion.

Note also that some have argued on the basis of the opening words of Luke iii that they must have constituted the original beginning of the gospel, and that the birth narratives are to be regarded as of later origin. On this subject see J. Gresham Machen, *The Virgin Birth of Christ*, 2nd edit., pp. 47 ff.

[2] Op. cit., p. 57. Permission to quote this passage has been kindly granted by the publishers, Harper & Brothers.

The prominence assigned to the Baptist is therefore not gained at the expense of Jesus; on the contrary, the greater the significance attached to John's mission, the greater the glory of the One whom he was sent to herald. And Luke's very readiness to allow the spotlight to rest upon John at the beginning of his ministry is another proof that Luke was not writing a secular biography with Jesus as his hero. Rather he is occupied here with his task of publishing the gospel of Jesus Christ which came to public expression in history with John's witness to, and baptism of, Jesus.[1]

This conclusion regarding the relation of the Baptist to the Christ within the gospel is confirmed by other significant Lucan testimony. Both the angelic annunciation of John's birth and the prophetic testimony of Zacharias after the event stress John's mission to prepare the way of 'the Lord.' He is 'to make ready for the Lord a people prepared for Him' (i. 17), and as 'the prophet of Most High' he is to 'go before the face of the Lord to make ready His ways' (i. 76). Even if the coming of the Lord referred to in these utterances should be regarded as an echo of Old Testament prophecies of the coming of the great day of God, rather than precisely and narrowly of the coming of the Messiah, the preparatory and subordinate character of John's mission would still be emphasized. Moreover, there can be no question that these two lines of prophecy converge in the New Testament: the coming of the Lord God and the coming of the messianic salvation are one. Not John but Jesus is the divine Messiah who accomplishes the redemption of Israel.

And in view of the prominence given to the Lordship of Jesus by Luke, both within the birth narratives and afterward, one cannot dismiss the thought that Luke actually has the Lord Jesus Himself in mind when he reports the declarations of the angel and of John's father concerning John's mission to make ready for the coming of the Lord. At any rate, Luke himself offers the most vivid and striking testimony of the fact that the Lord's Christ is Christ the Lord (cf. ii. 26 and ii. 11). And not only an angel of the Lord but Elizabeth, the mother of John, is a witness to the Lordship of Jesus. And John is represented as having prepared the

[1] Acts underscores the significant place occupied by the Baptist's ministry within the apostolic preaching. Cf. i. 22, x, 37, xiii. 24.

way for his mother's confession. This occurs in the account of the visit of Mary to Elizabeth about three months before the birth of John, a visit apparently occasioned by the declaration of the angel Gabriel, assuring Mary 'that no word of God shall be void of power,' that Elizabeth had conceived a son in her old age (i. 36 f.). Mary, who previously had asked, 'how shall this be, seeing I know not a man?' (i. 34), receives new assurance when she calls upon Elizabeth, for Elizabeth becomes the vehicle of the Holy Spirit in revealing the true relationship between their yet unborn sons:

'Blessed art thou among women
And blessed is the fruit of thy womb.
And whence is this to me,
That the mother of my Lord should come unto me.
For behold,
When the voice of thy salutation came into mine ears,
The babe leaped in my womb for joy.
And blessed is she that believed;
For there shall be a fulfilment of the things
Which have been spoken to her from the Lord.'

(i. 42–45.)

Thus John, before his birth, is represented as sensing that a momentous event was about to occur, and he shares in the joy which it was to spell to men. And his mother, responding to that impetus, in greeting Mary acknowledges her greater Son as her own Lord. The interweaving of the intimate histories of Mary and Elizabeth (cf. i. 24, 26, 36, 56), and their coming together for a visit of three months, are not told, therefore, to colour the narrative with charming details, or to satisfy curiosity as to the character of their mothers, or to hold the women up before us as examples of piety, or, and this least of all, to exalt Mary as 'the mother of God.' Mary and Elizabeth and John are present only because of the light that is focused by their actions and words upon Him who is acknowledged as having the right to bear the incomparably exalted name of Lord, which in the Greek Old Testament was used far and away most frequently as the name of God, the great Jehovah.

Other indications are not wanting that Luke, in spite of the prominence given to the Baptist, assigns him the role of servant in the house of the Lord. If Luke were really intending to ascribe to the Baptist a place of relative independence in relation to Christ, or even to dwell upon his significance as a secondary character in the origin and early development of Christian history, his silence with regard to certain aspects of John's career would be inscrutable. Most remarkable in this connection is the abruptness of his treatment of the baptism of Jesus:

> 'Now it came to pass, when all the people were baptized, that, Jesus also having been baptized, and praying, the heaven was opened, and the Holy Spirit descended in a bodily form, as a dove, upon Him, and a voice came out of heaven, Thou art my beloved Son; in Thee I am well pleased' (iii. 21, 22).

While both Matthew and Mark report the journey of Jesus from Galilee to the Jordan river for the baptism, Luke does not say anything concerning it. Jesus is simply there at the place of baptism. And His baptism is recorded in two words—by means of a genitive absolute participial construction, the reference to the baptism being incidental to the record of the descent of the Spirit and the acclamation of the heavenly voice. Since John's ministry as a preacher of the necessity of baptism and as an administrator of baptism has been prominently brought before the reader (iii. 3 ff., 16), it may be taken for granted that Luke thinks of him as the baptizer of Jesus. But it is extraordinary that exactly at the baptism of Jesus, where one might expect John at least to share some of the limelight with Jesus, he is not mentioned at all.[1]

That Luke is not characterized by a stronger biographical motif than the other evangelists appears also from his treatment of the close of John's career. He briefly concludes his record of the history of John by introducing, immediately before the reference to the baptism of Jesus, a notice of Herod's imprisonment of John (iii. 19, 20). This the other synoptics do not describe until much later in their accounts, at the point where they tell of

[1] In Acts the perspective remains basically the same. 'The baptism of John' in i. 22, might indeed refer to John's baptism of Jesus, but more probably it points broadly to the ministry of John. Acts x. 37, and xiii. 24, speak of the *preaching* of baptism, and x. 38, significantly states that 'God anointed him with the Holy Spirit and with power.'

John's execution (Mt. xiv. 1-12; Mk. vi. 14-29; but cf. Mt. iv. 12; Mk. i. 14). Since Jesus had not yet been baptized, Luke is evidently anticipating a later event. Luke also presupposes that John lived for some time after the beginnings of the ministry of Jesus (vii. 18 ff.). But Luke alone of the synoptists fails to tell the story of the death of John. This silence, like that concerning John's baptism of Jesus, provides eloquent testimony that John is not introduced for his own sake.[1]

We see, therefore, that John the Baptist, than whom there was no greater born among women (vii. 28), as well as the obscure Simeon, owes his place in the early chapters of Luke to the light that his testimony casts upon the significance of Jesus Christ. The contacts of these two men with the origin and early history of Jesus provide occasions for disclosures which interpret authoritatively the meaning of the stupendous event represented by the birth of Christ and His presence in the world.

Although, as previously stated, Luke views Christianity as a movement within the framework of world history, the secular interest of Luke must not be exaggerated. One may not, without careful qualifications, suppose that he self-consciously writes as 'the historian' of Christianity. As the selective character of Acts shows, he is not endeavouring to publish a history of the apostolic church. And the Gospel likewise provides many evidences of a choice of materials with a view to the publication of a distinctive testimony to Christ. His interest in the chronological setting of the commencement of the public phase of the gospel history, as demonstrated in the opening words of the third chapter, is by no means characteristic of his writing as a whole.

THE INTRODUCTION OF JESUS

These conclusions regarding the disposition and theme of the chapters Luke devotes to the historical beginnings of Christianity may be tested further as we finally consider briefly the manner in which Jesus Himself is introduced within the temporal framework of world history. Although chronological data of considerable

[1] In Lk. ix. 9, indeed, Luke reports Herod as saying: 'John I beheaded, but who is this about whom I hear such things?' However, the very incidental character of this reference to the death of the Baptist confirms our conclusion as to Luke's method.

interest occur, it is doubtful that they are presented because of secular or biographical interests.

The priestly activity of Zacharias is declared to have taken place 'in the days of Herod, king of Judæa' (i. 5). From the use of this phrase at the very beginning of the closely linked and integrated narration of the origins of John and Jesus, one is perhaps meant to infer that the birth of Christ also took place during the reign of Herod, as Matthew explicitly reports. But the fact remains that Luke does not provide explicit confirmation of Matthew's statement.

When Luke comes to the narration of the birth of Christ, he introduces a more precise secular reference, the reference to an enrolment made while Quirinius was governor over the province of Syria as a consequence of a decree of Caesar Augustus (ii. 1 f.). Still the interest in the mention of this event is not barely chronological. Luke's reason for referring to the enrolment is to indicate the historical occasion of the journey of Joseph and Mary from their home in northern Palestine to the town of Bethlehem where the Christ was to be born. And it is entirely in keeping with his literary method and style to describe that enrolment in concrete and precise terms. Whatever chronological knowledge one may glean from these references is gained quite incidentally. Since Caesar Augustus reigned for some forty years, from 27 B.C. to A.D. 14, not much specific knowledge is gained from the intimation that the enrolment followed a decree of this emperor. And the summary manner in which Luke speaks of the enrolment under Quirinius as a 'first enrolment,' without clarifying whatever other enrolment or enrolments may have been in view, furnishes the reader, at least the modern one, with precious little exact information as to the time when this enrolment, and consequently when the birth of Christ, took place.[1]

There remains the fascinating temporal reference in Lk. iii. 23 to the commencement of the public ministry of Jesus in connection with which Luke states that Jesus was approximately thirty years of age. There are difficulties in the translation of this statement due largely to the fact that the participle 'beginning' is

[1] On the exegetical and historical questions connected with Lk. ii. 2, cf. especially Armstrong, 'Chronology of the N.T.', in ISBE, I, pp. 404 f.; Machen, op. cit., pp. 239 ff.

unqualified, but the most natural rendering is that in which the participle is understood as referring to the inauguration of the public ministry of Christ: 'Jesus Himself, when He began, was about thirty years of age.' As the day when 'the word of God came to John,' the day of 'his showing to Israel' (iii. 1 f., i. 80), marked the dawn of a new epoch, so the day when Christ entered upon His work could be designated, in a more absolute sense, as *the beginning*. In spite of the more formal introduction of the beginning of John's ministry in contrast to the rather bare and somewhat abrupt reference to Jesus' 'beginning,' Luke unmistakably marks the latter as of incomparably greater moment. It is the moment when He who has been acclaimed by a heavenly voice as the beloved Son of God (iii. 22) is about to undertake the fulfilment of His mission.[1]

Although, then, the intimation that Jesus was about thirty years of age at the commencement of His public ministry is a chronological datum of the utmost interest it can hardly be regarded as presented with a view to giving us a precise framework of the course of His life. Otherwise Luke could hardly have failed to state later on the age of Jesus at His death.[2] Perhaps Luke had in mind only the fact that at the time He entered upon His public work He had reached mature manhood; but this remains uncertain.[3]

Our general conclusion with regard to the approach of the early chapters of Luke is, accordingly, that biographical and

[1] On the interpretation of v. 23, cf. Plummer, ad loc.; Machen, op. cit., p. 53. See also Acts i. 22, and x. 37, where the beginning of Jesus' action is also intimately associated with John's career. The rendering of the AV: 'And Jesus Himself began to be about thirty years of age . . .' is to be rejected as reading into the Greek more than it says, and as not being wholly intelligible. The RV furnishes a more natural construction: 'And Jesus himself, when he began *to teach*, was about thirty years of age . . .' However, there is no good reason for restricting the ministry to teaching activity. The RSV paraphrases the view taken here: 'Jesus, when he began his ministry, was about thirty years of age. . . .'

[2] An implication of some importance for the chronology of the life of Jesus is that His ministry must have lasted considerably over a year. If Luke supposed that Jesus had completed His ministry when He was still about thirty years of age, he would hardly have expressed himself as he does. Cf. Zahn, *Einleitung*, II, p. 443 (E.T., III, p. 168); *Kommentar* (1913), pp. 204 f.; Schmidt, *Rahmen*, pp. 30 f. Ogg, op. cit., pp. 13 ff. argues against the conclusiveness of this reasoning, but not very impressively.

[3] Turner, op. cit., p. 405, opposed the notion that the maturity of Jesus at the commencement of His public ministry is in view.

secular interests are wholly or almost completely absent, and that Luke is everywhere an evangelist. He is demonstrating that, from the very beginning of the life of Jesus, the facts of His life, and Jesus as the great fact, were interpreted authoritatively as constituting glad tidings of salvation. One may freely acknowledge, then, that his interest is theological and christological since his entire message is presented in terms of divine action and revelation, and is occupied with the proclamation of Jesus as the divine Messiah. But it is crucial to a proper estimate of the Lucan philosophy of history not to regard the christological and the historical as mutually exclusive. Though he does not write as a secular historian, Luke gives evidence at every point of being concerned with historical fact and takes great pains to assure his readers that he is qualified to provide them with reliable information concerning what had taken place. The concept of Messiahship is historical as well as theological; the Anointed of the Lord is One whose *coming* into the world constitutes the single theme of the revelation of both covenants, and it is that aspect of the manifestation of the Christ which is the very foundation of the gospel.

CHAPTER IV

PREACHING AND CONFLICT AT NAZARETH

THE appearance of Jesus in Nazareth 'where he was brought up,' and his rejection there on the part of his fellow townsmen, comprise one of the most arresting features of the entire Lucan portrayal of the public ministry. This narrative, in view of its position at the very beginning of the story of the Galilean activity, as the first concrete report of the message of Jesus and of the impact which He made upon His hearers, is somewhat plausibly regarded by many students of Luke as deliberately chosen to present the leading motifs of the Gospel. The message is solemnly introduced in the prophetic words of Isaiah:

'The Spirit of the Lord is upon me,
Because He anointed Me to preach good tidings to the poor:
He hath sent Me to proclaim release to the captives,
And recovering of sight to the blind,
To set at liberty them that are bruised,
To proclaim the acceptable year of the Lord.'

(iv. 18, 19.)

The realization of the gospel in history is announced by Jesus in completely unambiguous terms: 'Today this scripture is fulfilled in your hearing!' Although 'the words of grace which proceeded out of His mouth' are not set down in detail, the text quoted from the Old Testament and its immediate historical application are so specific that this first Lucan report of the proclamation of Jesus appears to serve as an inaugural address. But hard upon the completion of the address comes the denouement in terms of rationalizing doubt, offence, rejection, wrath and murderous hate. Thus Luke at once discloses that the good tidings of grace and liberty tragically failed to win the universal acclaim and acceptance which their intrinsic meaning and validity justified and demanded.

Nor is the originality of the Lucan introduction of Jesus qualified decisively by the consideration that Matthew and Mark also contain vivid accounts of the rejection at Nazareth. Indeed, in spite of the broad correspondence of the three synoptic accounts, and to an extent because of this very correspondence, the distinctive features in Luke tend to emphasize, rather than to detract from, the novelty of his narration. Matthew and Mark wait until near the close of their accounts of the Galilean ministry to introduce the story of the unbelief of His fellow Nazarenes (Mt. xiii. 53 ff.; Mk. vi. 1 ff.). In contrast Luke appears very bold in sounding this sombre note at this very early point, even before he has dwelt triumphantly upon the favour with which Jesus was received by many. Moreover, the message of Jesus at Nazareth is expressed in distinctive terms. Here surely he is not following a stereotyped pattern which had been formed by earlier evangelists. No one will dispute the conclusion, accordingly, that Lk. iv. 16-30 provides a most fascinating instance of the distinctiveness of Luke, and that it has most important bearings upon one's understanding of the public ministry as a whole.

As a background for the study of this incident, one may note with advantage the modern critical estimate of Luke's procedure at this point. Generally speaking, his treatment of the episode at Nazareth has not served to commend his Gospel to modern historical critics. The charge is frequently made that Luke betrays here a lack of historical objectivity. Either deliberately or unconsciously he is thought to have revealed his own special insights and to have disclosed his peculiar bias. The modern exponents of the two-document theory of Gospel origins, in particular, view these materials as proof of a radical manipulation of the Christian tradition. J. M. Creed, for example, maintains that Luke took the narrative found in Mark vi as the foundation 'for a representative and symbolic scene to open the public ministry of Jesus,' and that Luke himself 'is mainly responsible for the section as it stands.' He further says:

> 'The narrative must not be pressed. Its real function is to introduce the main *motifs* which are to recur throughout the Gospel and the Acts, and this it does with great effect: the gospel to the poor is preached by Jesus in His home and rejected. The rejection by Nazareth foreshadows the rejection by the Jewish people and the subsequent universal mission of the Church.'[1]

[1] Op. cit., pp. 65, 66. Cf. also R. H. Lightfoot, *History and Interpretation in the Gospels*, pp. 182 ff., 196 f., 199 f., 202.

Other students of Luke, like Easton and William Manson, though regarding the evangelist as essentially an editor rather than as the creator of new forms of tradition, likewise disparage Luke's account. The evangelist is thought, on their view, to have elaborated upon the incident recorded in Mark. Both the position which the incident occupies within the framework of the ministry of Christ and the distinctive formulation of the message of Jesus are thought to demonstrate that Mark is more reliable.[1]

THE HISTORICAL SETTING

The question why Luke begins the narration of the public ministry with the incident at Nazareth must be examined because of its bearing upon the larger question of the distinctiveness of Luke's witness to Christ. One aspect of the problem is whether Luke actually intended to present the address at Nazareth as an inaugural discourse or as programmatic, and thus as indicative of his special interests and emphases.

These matters require an examination of the historical setting of the incident in relation to the Matthaean and Marcan data. We shall help to clear the atmosphere if, first of all, we face the question whether there may not have been two appearances in Nazareth, one near the beginning of the Galilean ministry, reported by Luke, and a second near its close, recorded by Matthew and Mark. Mark indeed says nothing of a visit to Nazareth until the account in chapter vi, and he may appear to centre the earliest activity in Capernaum. Nevertheless, in view of the summary description of activity in Galilee in Mk. i. 14 f. ('Now after that John was delivered up, Jesus came into Galilee, preaching the gospel of God, and saying, The time is fulfilled, and the kingdom of heaven is at hand: repent ye, and believe in the gospel'), and the episodic character of Mark's narrative as a whole, the possibility of a ministry in Nazareth before the activity in Capernaum cannot be excluded.[2] Matthew indeed solemnly indicates that Capernaum was the centre of Jesus' early activity, but he explicitly mentions a stay in *Nazara* (the same

[1] In the Commentaries, ad loc.

[2] William Manson, MC, p. 40, is not on solid ground when he avers that 'Mark definitely locates the earliest activities of Jesus in Capernaum. . . .' Mark does not speak of 'the earliest activities' in point of time.

distinctive form that Luke employed in iv. 16) before He went to Capernaum, without, however, relating anything that happened in Nazara, or stating what occasioned His departure (Mt. iv. 13 ff). So far as the pertinent evidence in Matthew and Mark go therefore, it is entirely possible to maintain that Luke reports here a significant incident not mentioned by the other evangelists, and that he may have omitted reference to a later rejection at Nazareth in the interest of brevity and in view of his earlier inclusion of a similar narrative.[1]

To allow for the possibility of two distinct instances of rejection at Nazareth, however, is not tantamount to the conclusion that the evidence requires us to assume two such incidents, or that it encourages us, on the whole, to accept that as a solution of the problem. If attention is now turned to the Lucan data which bear upon the decision, we may determine whether this Gospel allows of, and perhaps even suggests, the conclusion that the appearance in Nazareth which it describes may legitimately be regarded as having taken place considerably after the commencement of the public ministry in Galilee.

Most illuminating is the observation that, prior to the narrative reporting what occurred at Nazareth, Luke speaks quite independently of the Galilean ministry:

> 'And Jesus returned in the power of the Spirit into Galilee: and a fame went out concerning Him through all the region round about. And He taught in their synagogues, being glorified of all' (Lk. iv. 14 f.).

He tells, therefore, quite without reference to Nazareth, of a period of activity in Galilee, in which Jesus was busy teaching in the synagogues, and became well known.[2] It appears therefore

[1] Advocates of the Four-document Theory maintain approximately this same viewpoint, except for the significant difference that they regard all the narratives as pointing back to a single historical event. They assert that the final editor of the Gospel, when he came to interpolate portions of Mark into Proto-Luke, did not introduce Mk. vi. 1-6, because an account of the rejection at Nazareth already occupied a position at the beginning of the narrative of activity in Galilee as found in Proto-Luke, which he was principally following. Cf. Streeter, op. cit., pp. 209 f.; Taylor, *Behind the Third Gospel*, p. 142, p. 192.

[2] Cf. also iv. 16, where Luke reports that Jesus came to Nazareth, and 'entered, as His custom was, into the synagogue on the sabbath day.' The reference must be to His custom of entering the synagogues of Galilee on the sabbath day.

that the entrance into the synagogue at Nazareth, like His ministry in Capernaum reported in Lk. iv. 31 ff., is presented as an instance, but not necessarily the first instance, of preaching in Galilee. When, following the survey of activity in Capernaum, Luke reports Jesus as saying, 'I must preach the gospel of the kingdom to other cities also' (iv. 43), and follows this with the intimation that, as a matter of fact, 'Jesus was preaching in the synagogues of Judæa' (iv. 44) we have further evidence that Luke does not intend to supply his readers with an itinerary of Jesus' mission in Galilee. The activity in Nazareth and in Capernaum are presented as illustrative of the preaching and healing ministry of Jesus as a whole. In effect, therefore, he does not say more than that, *in the course of Jesus' ministry in the synagogues of Galilee, He also preached in the synagogue at Nazareth.* He by no means says or implies that the Galilean ministry began at Nazareth, or that the address there was His inaugural proclamation.[1]

The general contextual considerations, accordingly, allow definitely for the possibility that the incident at Nazareth took place relatively late in the Galilean ministry, but do not bring to a decision what Luke actually thought on the matter. The question appears to be settled once for all, however, by a reference to Capernaum in the discourse of Jesus at Nazareth. In reply to the exclamation, 'Is not this Joseph's son?' Jesus said:

> 'Doubtless ye will say unto Me this parable, Physician, heal thyself: Whatsoever we have heard done at Capernaum, do also here in Thine own country' (iv. 23).

How can these words be understood unless all the while Luke has been presupposing a previous period of activity in Capernaum? The plain implication seems to be that his hearers at Nazareth are understood by Jesus as being informed concerning his previous activity in Capernaum.[2]

[1] The only detail which might appear to establish chronological sequence between the appearances in Nazareth and in Capernaum is the use of the verb κατῆλθεν in iv. 31, which would appropriately describe a journey from the higher ground at Nazareth to Capernaum on the sea shore. But this may not be pressed. It may mean merely 'arrive'. See MM; Liddell and Scott, *Greek-English Lexicon*, 1940; cf. Plummer, ad loc.

[2] Cf. Augustine, *Harmony of the Evangelists*, II, xliii (90): Migne, *Pat. Lat.* xxxiv. 1121 f.; Easton; Creed; Greijdanus.

But even this specific mention of Capernaum is thought by Wellhausen not to clinch the matter.[1] According to Wellhausen, Luke represents the residents of Nazareth as manifesting a positively favourable attitude toward Jesus at first, and that only the final remarks provoked them to wrath. The favourable attitude is thought to be displayed particularly in the words that 'all bare him witness, and wondered at the words of grace which proceeded out of his mouth' (v. 22).[2] Their question, 'Is not this Joseph's son?' on this view merely indicates surprise, not a basic scepticism or hostility. And Jesus' words that follow (verses 23 ff.) are judged by Wellhausen to intimate that He cannot rejoice in their present favourable attitude since He knows that *at some future time* their attitude will change. When Jesus says, 'Doubtless *ye will say* unto Me this parable, Physician, heal thyself: whatsoever we have heard done at Capernaum, do also here in Thine own country,' He is speaking of a future attitude to be disclosed in what they would say to taunt and ridicule Him. The implication of Luke's report is, accordingly, that Jesus anticipates a future activity in Capernaum and beyond that another visit to Nazareth when He would be mocked. Wellhausen also implies that Luke's use of traditional materials at this point provides a particularly crass example of the failure of an editor to observe the full consequence of a transposition, for Luke is supposed to anticipate the narrative of Mk. vi and yet to retain the thought of its futurity.

Although the passage admittedly is not without exegetical difficulty due largely to the problem of reaching certainty concerning continuity and transition in thought and reaction, the view of Wellhausen must be rejected as raising grave difficulties and as offering no really satisfactory solution of detailed questions. In general his view attributes extreme clumsiness to Luke, and presupposes that the constituent elements of the Lucan narrative can be harmonized with each other only on the assumption that there has been profound confusion concerning the actual facts. Thus the difficulty of arriving at an integrated interpretation is greatly exaggerated. Moreover, Wellhausen's view is itself beset by insuperable exegetical obstacles.

[1] *Evangelien, Das Evangelium Lucae*, 1904, pp. 8 ff. Cf. also Klostermann, HBNT, ad loc.

[2] The RSV translates: 'And all spoke well of him, and wondered at the gracious words which proceeded out of his mouth.' Cf. J. W. Bowman, *The Intention of Jesus*, 1943, pp. 92 ff.

The decision will turn mainly about the question of the propriety of interpreting the future 'ye will say' of a reaction of His hearers at some future date when Jesus would return to Nazareth. Even the general tone of the address, with its note of urgency and timeliness, suggests that Jesus is concerned with the immediate response of His hearers, rather than, more casually, with an eventual and rather remote situation. Moreover, the Lucan account is perfectly clear in disclosing that the reaction of hostility is not remote, for a most conspicuous feature of his narrative is that they were filled with murderous wrath before He had concluded speaking (v. 28). *When the prediction of hostility finds immediate fulfilment, is it not far-fetched to insist that Luke has in mind a remote outbreak of opposition in Nazareth, concerning which Luke actually reports nothing?*

Moreover, the view that the hostility manifested at the end of Jesus' discourse constitutes a reversal of an earlier positively favourable attitude is open to serious question. The wonder at the words of grace spoken by Jesus may seem indeed to point in that direction. But their state of wonder may not be isolated from the question, 'Is not this Joseph's son?' which immediately follows and is presented as a further disclosure of their reaction. This question is shown to manifest an attitude which Jesus felt called upon to rebuke. The continuity of question and answer demonstrates that Jesus anticipates that they are about to demand a display of miraculous power. And to this demand He was unwilling to respond. The transition from the words of His hearers to Jesus' own reply is therefore somewhat abrupt, but the attentive reader is given a sufficient intimation of the tone of their reply by Jesus' own interpretation of it.

The parallelism with Mark, moreover, is greater than appears at first sight, and serves to set the reaction of the Nazarenes in a clearer perspective. Mark also reports their wonder at His teaching: 'many hearing him were astonished, saying, Whence hath this man these things? and, What is the wisdom that is given unto this man, and what mean such mighty works wrought by his hands? Is not this the carpenter, the son of Mary, and brother of James, and Joses, and Judas, and Simon? and are not his sisters here with us?' (vi. 2, 3; cf. Mt. xiii. 54-56). But Mark immediately adds, 'And they were offended in Him' and soon adds that

Jesus 'marvelled because of their unbelief' (vi. 4-6; cf. Mt. xiii. 57). If Mark regards the astonishment evoked by the teaching and deeds of Jesus as being quite consonant with the offence and unbelief that came to immediate expression, may Luke be confidently judged to have in view two divergent attitudes when he speaks of their wonder at His teaching and of their taunting and wrathful reaction? The offence and unbelief of which Mark speaks are quite as negative as the reactions indicated by Luke, and hence are introduced fully as abruptly.[1] But the general disposition of Mark's narrative shows that the abruptness is more semblance than reality. Jewish hearers might marvel and be astonished at Jesus' proclamation of the dawn of the messianic salvation, which they might well acknowledge to have significant points of contact with their own eschatological outlook, and yet they might take offence because of the more or less open claim of Jesus to be associated intimately with its manifestation. That the kingdom of which the prophets spoke was coming was a message which might strike a responsive chord; that Jesus, who seemed to them to belong to their everyday existence in Nazareth, should be somehow responsible for it was quite a different matter. At this point, as later, it was the place occupied by Jesus within the gospel of the kingdom that caused men to stumble; but in the happenings at Nazareth the offence was accelerated and aggravated by their arrogant assurance that He who was of their number could not possibly wear the mantle of God's special minister.

My general conclusion, therefore, is that there is no need to resort to Wellhausen's extreme exegetical and critical procedures, and that the reference to previous activity in Capernaum in Lk. iv. 23 is adequately and naturally accounted for by the broad characterization of the Galilean ministry with which Luke begins his narrative of the public ministry of Jesus (iv. 14 f.). The activity in Nazareth is not described as inaugurating the public activity, and the address in the synagogue there may not precisely be characterized as the inaugural address of Jesus. All that may be said firmly is that it is Luke's first detailed account of Jesus' ministry. When one once recognizes that Luke's aim is not to tell

[1] Creed says that Luke softens Mark's 'offence,' but adds that 'here too we are probably meant to discover an undertone of indignation to which Jesus replies in the following verses.' He adds that 'in any case a very awkward transition is involved.'

in exact detail how Jesus' ministry in Galilee began, but only to illustrate its beginnings, it is no longer possible to insist that Luke intended to imply that the activity in Nazareth preceded that in Capernaum.

Nevertheless, the question as to what dictated the order of presentation remains to be considered. The answer may well be that, from among the various instances of preaching in the synagogues of Galilee, Luke selected the preaching at Nazareth because it could serve to present in brief compass some of the most significant features of the claims of Christ. To say that it is programmatic is misleading because, in spite of the many facets of its contents, it does not serve to sum up the distinctive testimony of Luke to Christ. For example, the full impact of the positive disclosure of Jesus' messianic claims is not realized in the manifestation at Nazareth. Nor does the place occupied in the Gospel by the parousia of Christ and the distinctly eschatological manifestation of the kingdom of God come to expression here. Nevertheless, conspicuous elements of the estimate of Christ which Luke is concerned to publish come vividly to view in the arresting account of what happened at Nazareth.

THE MESSAGE OF THE KINGDOM

The consideration of the historical setting of the appearance of Jesus at Nazareth has inevitably involved reflection upon certain aspects of Jesus' teaching there. It has appeared that it was in the course of His preaching the good tidings of the kingdom of God that He came to Nazareth (iv. 43 f.), and hence the actual proclamation there may advantageously be considered in the larger perspective of the message of the kingdom of God. The reaction to this message, of which some notice has already been taken, indicates that there was a personal aspect to the message of Jesus which provoked strong personal antagonism. And thus, in addition to the theme of the coming of the kingdom in the narrower sense, the question as to who Jesus claimed to be and how He conceived of His relation to the coming of the kingdom —in short, the christological question—is thrust into the foreground. These two interrelated themes—the coming of the kingdom and the coming of the Christ—will serve to place the varied contents of the preaching at Nazareth in sharpest relief.

That Luke, himself a Gentile and presumably writing with the Gentile world chiefly in view, introduces Jesus as reading from the Old Testament and as indicating that He had come to proclaim the fact of its fulfilment offers convincing evidence that Christianity according to Luke was not a new religion, but rather one whose foundations were established in what stood written in the Scriptures. Shortly before the ascension the risen Christ is reported as declaring that 'all things must needs be fulfilled, which are written in the law of Moses, and the prophets, and the psalms, concerning me' (Lk. xxiv. 44). Here in Lk. iv, at the beginning of His public ministry, Jesus is introduced as teaching that the necessary fulfilment of the Scriptures had already begun, indeed that it was taking place at the very moment that they heard the Scripture read. Although in the birth narratives (as has been demonstrated in the preceding chapter), the accent falls upon revelation contemporaneous with the momentous event of the birth of Christ, Luke shows here, beyond the shadow of a doubt, that the Old Testament revelation formed an integral aspect of the gospel proclamation. Luke no more than any other New Testament writer allows for the judgment that the Old Testament was expendable. Nor is the basic thought merely that Christianity would be unintelligible apart from an understanding of the manner in which its historical environment had been conditioned by the history of Israel and the message of its prophets and wise men. The Old Testament Scriptures were viewed as being themselves divinely given and of divine authority. Moreover, solid ground is reached only when there is recognition of the fact that Luke shares the philosophy of the history of revelation and redemption which distinguishes between the divine action and word in the old and new covenants. Thus only is there a perception of the diversity of the old and the new orders, a difference expressed oftentimes and perhaps most simply as one of prophecy and fulfilment. And thus only is justice done to the fact that the two covenants are ultimately considered one, and that only one religion is revealed in the Scriptures, only one way of salvation, as there is but one God who deals with sinners, and has declared and accomplished his purposes of righteousness and grace, in the old order as well as in the new.

The passage read by Christ shares the eschatological perspective of the Old Testament, recognized pervasively in the New, which envisages the dawn of a new day through the intervention of God in history. This outlook finds expression within the Old Testament in various forms which converge in the New Testament historical revelation: it is described in terms of the coming of the Lord, or of the coming of the Lord's Anointed, or of the outpouring of the divine Spirit. The language quoted by our Lord from Isaiah gives vivid expression to the hope of a new order of righteousness to be established by God and proclaimed by One who should be qualified to proclaim it by an anointing of the Spirit of the Lord.

That Jesus here proclaims the arrival of the new order of righteousness prophesied by Isaiah is evident even from a superficial reading of Luke's narrative, and there is apparently widespread agreement among modern interpreters of the Gospel on this point. But when one proceeds from general characterizations to more particular delineations of the exact nature of the kingdom of God as taught in Luke, and in the other writings of the New Testament, one encounters profound differences of judgment, ranging all the way from the view that the kingdom is essentially a moral order realized through human co-operation to the position that it has no point of contact whatsoever with this world order, and is to be realized solely by divine action. The issue at stake here—what the kingdom of God really is, how it confronts us, what it demands of us—is most basic to an understanding of the message of Jesus, more basic than the question often asked prematurely as to *the time* of the coming of the kingdom. This issue must be faced now as we study Luke's first record of the preaching of Jesus: it is an issue that remains urgent right throughout the study of the Gospel.

Progress towards a solution can be expected only if the Isaianic language is construed in its larger context. That the prophet presents, in the language quoted by Jesus, a gospel for the poor, the prisoner, the blind and the oppressed; that he proclaims righteousness and deliverance to men in misery and distress—these facts are inescapable. But exactly what does Isaiah mean by the poor and the oppressed, and how does he conceive that their needs will be met? We have become familiar with the claims that the prophets, and Jesus as standing in their tradition, proclaimed a social gospel, a gospel designed for the poor and afflicted of this world and aiming at the amelioration of their conditions. And it is not surprising that the preaching at Nazareth should be cited as offering proof that the Jesus of 'the social gospel' is the Jesus of the Gospels. Is there, however, any actual basis for this far-reaching conclusion? Does not the Isaianic analysis of the need of men and how this need is supplied actually point in a different direction?

The beneficent acts which are proclaimed by the anointed of the Lord are not brought before the reader of Isaiah for the first time in chapter lxi, but have been mentioned before especially in contexts where the Servant of the Lord has been introduced. Thus the stately forty-second chapter which begins

> 'Behold my servant whom I uphold;
> My chosen, in whom my soul delighteth;
> I have put my Spirit upon him;
> He will bring forth judgment to the Gentiles.'
>
> (Is. xlii. 1.)

proceeds soon with the declaration

> 'I the Lord have called thee in righteousness,
> And will hold thine hand,
> And will keep thee,
> And give thee for a covenant of the people,
> For a light of the Gentiles;
> To open the blind eyes,
> To bring out the prisoners from the dungeon,
> And them that sit in darkness out of the prison-house.'
>
> (Is. xlii. 6 f.)

Previously Isaiah had predicted the deliverance of the people in these terms:

> 'And in that day shall the deaf hear the words of the book,
> And the eyes of the blind shall see out of obscurity and out of darkness.
> The meek also shall increase their joy in the Lord,
> And the poor among men shall rejoice in the Holy One of Israel.'
>
> (Is. xxix. 18 f.)

The words quoted from Is. lxi come therefore as a reiteration and reinforcement of the message of the redemption of the people of God which has been the dominant theme of the evangelical prophet.

Who, then, are the poor and how are they delivered from poverty? We must certainly avoid the extreme of supposing that Isaiah's contemplation of the poor disregards the social conditions of his time and has in view only the spiritual state of Israel. The truly pious man is emphatically not one who, though scrupulous with regard to all the formal observances of religion, neglects the requirements of mercy; the Lord is indignant with such and asks

'Is not this the fast that I have chosen?
To loose the bonds of wickedness,
To undo the bands of the yoke,
And to let the oppressed go free,
And that ye break every yoke?
Is it not to deal thy bread to the hungry,
And that thou bring the poor that are cast out to thy house?'
(Is. lviii. 6, 7a.)

But it is, nevertheless, particularly the *poor of God's people* that are in view, and it is against those who have been appointed to rule righteously that the wrath of God is pronounced:

'The Lord will enter into judgment
With the elders of his people and the princes thereof:
It is ye that have eaten up the vineyard;
The spoil of the poor is in your houses:
What mean ye that ye crush my people,
And grind the face of the poor?
Saith the Lord, the Lord of hosts.'
(iii. 14 f.; cf. x. 1, 2.)

These acts of unrighteousness, this grinding of the face of the poor, are, therefore, roundly condemned, and men are called upon to repent of their wicked exploitation and discrimination. But the analysis of the social situation is nevertheless not one which contemplates that a 'new deal' will be realized for the poor through a process of reform from within. On the contrary the gospel of the prophet points to the Holy One of Israel as the One who alone will effect a radical change in the fortunes of the poor. And the transformation that is promised is viewed as part of a radical and thoroughgoing renewal of the present order:

> 'The poor and needy seek water and there is none,
> And their tongue faileth for thirst;
> I the Lord will answer them,
> I the God of Israel will not forsake them.
> I will open rivers on the bare heights,
> And fountains in the midst of the valleys:
> I will make the wilderness a pool of water,
> And the dry land springs of water.
> I will plant in the wilderness the cedar,
> The acacia tree, and the myrtle, and the oil tree;
> I will set in the desert the fir-tree,
> The pine, and the box-tree together:
> That they may see, and know, and consider, and understand together,
> That the hand of the Lord hath done this,
> And the Holy One of Israel hath created it.'
>
> (Is. xli. 17-20.)

As accomplished by the Lord who insists that men shall recognize that He and He alone has done it (cf. also xlviii. 5), this announcement of salvation inevitably cannot have in view that the poor of the earth, as such, simply because of their poverty, will be without want. The poor who ultimately will rejoice in the Holy One of Israel are the meek who shall increase their joy in the Lord, while 'they that watch for iniquity are cut off' (xxix. 19 f.). In short, the age of transformation will be the portion of a transformed people.

The one anointed with the Lord's Spirit next declares that He has been sent 'to proclaim release to the captives.' Here it is even clearer than in the instance of Isaiah's contemplation of the poor that compassionate concern is being shown for the covenant children of God. The captivity and bondage of Israel as God's people and their deliverance from their oppressors by the Mighty One of Jacob constitute one of the most significant aspects of the prophetic doctrine of the coming salvation.

'Awake, awake, put on thy strength, O Zion;
Put on thy beautiful garments, O Jerusalem, the holy city;
For henceforth there shall no more come into thee
The uncircumcised and the unclean.
Shake thyself from the dust;
Arise, sit on thy throne, O Jerusalem;
Loose thyself from the bands of thy neck,
O captive daughter of Zion.
For thus saith the Lord,
Ye were sold for nought;
And ye shall be redeemed without money.
For thus saith the Lord God,
My people went down at the first into Egypt to sojourn there;
And the Assyrian hath oppressed them without cause.
Now, therefore, what do I here, saith the Lord,
Seeing that My people is taken away for nought?
They that rule over them do howl, saith the Lord,
And My name continually all the day is blasphemed.
Therefore My people shall know My name;
Therefore they shall know in that day
That I am He that doth speak;
Behold it is I.'

(Is. lii. 1-6, A.R.V.; cf. xlix. 8-13; 22 ff., 24 ff.)

Though Isaiah stirs the consciences of the people to 'loose the bonds of wickedness' (lviii. 6), the proclamation of release to the captives cannot have precisely in view the plight of outcasts, and least of all the misery of men who are imprisoned because of their own iniquity. Not the suffering of sinful men as such is the basic cause of God's action, but its basis is rather His contemplation of the fact that the captivity of His people causes His enemies to blaspheme and His recollection of the covenant which He has mercifully established with Israel.

Following the text of the Septuagint, as the quotation in Luke rather closely does throughout, mention is next made of 'the recovering of sight to the blind.' This feature of Isaiah's gospel might be understood quite literally; so indeed our Lord has evidently understood it, as reported by both Luke and Matthew, when He alludes to this language assuring John the Baptist that

He was indeed the one that should come (Lk. vii. 22; Mt. xi. 5). But even in the Gospels the historical miracles are not viewed as merely isolated acts of mercy and beneficence, but as signs of the inbreaking of the promised rule of God. And there can be little doubt that Isaiah has pre-eminently in view the divine action in removing the spiritual blindness. This blindness is specifically ascribed to Israel as a nation:

We look for light, but behold, darkness;
For brightness, but we walk in obscurity.
We grope for the wall like the blind,
Yea, we grope as they that have no eyes:
We stumble at noonday as in the twilight . . .
We look for judgment, but there is none;
For salvation, but it is far off from us.
For our transgressions are multiplied before Thee,
And our sins testify against us:
For our transgressions are with us,
And as for our iniquities, we know them:
In transgressing and denying the Lord,
And turning away from following our God,
Speaking oppression and revolt,
Conceiving and uttering from the heart words of falsehood.
And judgment is turned away backward,
And righteousness standeth afar off.
For truth is fallen in the street,
And uprightness cannot enter.'

(Is. lix. 9-14.)

And considering Israel as the servant of the Lord, he says:

'Who is blind, but My servant?
Or deaf, as My messenger that I send?
Who is blind as he that is at peace with Me,
And blind as the Lord's servant?
Thou seest many things, but thou observest not;
His ears are open, but he heareth not.'

(Is. xlii. 19-20.)

When, therefore, the blessed future of the people of God is realized, when 'the ransomed of the Lord shall return, and come with singing unto Zion; and everlasting joy shall be upon their heads,' 'the eyes of the blind shall be opened, and the ears of the deaf shall be unstopped' (Is. xxxv. 5, 10). Its own eyes opened, Israel shall be 'for a light to the Gentiles' (xlii. 6 f., xlix. 6).

'To set at liberty them that are bruised' is derived from Is. lviii. 6, where it is mentioned among the things pertaining to true religion. But like the call to minister to the poor, it must be understood as ultimately realizable only through the divine action of salvation. Isaiah does not provide the specific linguistic background for the interpretation of this statement which has been observed in the other clauses. The verb appears to be used in addition only in Is. xlii. 4, but evidently in a different sense. Dt. xxviii. 33, speaking of the consequences of disobedience, states that 'thou shalt be only *oppressed* and crushed away' (the same verb is used in both the Hebrew and the LXX as in the texts of Is. lviii. 6), and thus serves to establish the antithesis of judgment and salvation. In spite of the absence within Isaiah of the exact terminology used in this clause, the contextual thought of breaking every oppressive yoke is not novel. For example, in Is. xiv. 25, the Lord of Hosts swears that 'I will break the Assyrian in My land; then shall his yoke depart from off them, and his burden depart from off their shoulder.' This thought is closely related to that of the release of captives.[1]

If any doubt remains that the prophetic message quoted by our Lord at Nazareth had in view the eschatological salvation of the new age to come, that vanishes when one takes note of the concluding feature of the proclamation: the annunciation of 'the acceptable year of the Lord.' Thus the enactment and observance of the year of Jubilee, when liberty should be proclaimed throughout the land unto all the inhabitants thereof, and old arrangements would be restored and new beginnings made (Lv. xxv. 10 ff.,

[1] Cf. Ezk. xxx. 18, xxxiv, 27, where the same word for yoke appears as in Is. lviii. 6, and reference is made to the Lord's breaking the yoke of the enemies of His people.

On the combination of Is. lviii. 6, with the opening words of Is. lxi, cf. I Abrahams, *Studies in Pharisaism and the Gospels*, First Series, 1917, pp. 8 f.: 'The right to "skip" while reading the prophets was well attested (*Mishnah*, *Megilla*, iv. 4). Being written on a Scroll, the two passages might easily be open together, and Jesus, in accordance with what at all events became a usual Rabbinic device, intended to use both texts as the key to His exposition.' The larger context in which 'The Freedom of the Synagogue' is discussed is also of interest.

xxvii. 24), is utilized to characterize the new order as a time of grace and liberty (cf. Je. xxxiv. 8–10; Ezk. xlvi. 17).

In general, then, Isaiah views the people as in a state of sin and misery, in poverty and oppression, in bondage and darkness. But a new day of salvation and deliverance is promised, a day when righteousness will reign supreme. Israel is implicated in the evil because of her perversity, and thus her state of misery constitutes a just judgment upon her and the deliverance in view demands that she turn her back upon her sin and return unto God. Nevertheless, the God who saves Israel is not like unto men that He should bargain with them, or await their response before manifesting His favour, but freely manifests His saving work, telling beforehand what He will do that none may take His work for granted or attribute it to an idol, and that all may acknowledge that God is sovereign in His saving acts.

Is not Isaiah's delineation of the coming kingdom of God the very pattern of the kingdom as it is proclaimed by our Lord and as it begins to come to realization through His mighty deeds?

THE KINGDOM AND THE ANOINTED ONE

In addition to the basic subject of the meaning of the coming of the kingdom of God according to Jesus Christ, the Lucan narrative brings before us a still more challenging question, perhaps the most controversial of all contemporaneous questions relating to the interpretation of the Gospels: What relation does Jesus Christ Himself sustain, according to His own claims, to the manifestation of the rule of God?

In general modern criticism has tended to reduce the role of Christ to that of a mere herald. The older liberalism affirmed in the words of Harnack that 'The gospel, as Jesus proclaimed it, has to do with the Father only and not with the Son,' thus excluding Him from an integral place within the gospel. Yet Harnack went on to say that 'He was its personal realization and its strength, and this He is felt to be still,'[1] thereby giving expression to the motif that, after all, the historic personality of Jesus was a factor which was indispensable to the liberals. On this view the historicity of the messianic consciousness of Jesus was affirmed

[1] *Das Wesen des Christentums*, 1901, pp. 91 f. (*What is Christianity?*, p. 144, p. 145).

in the abstract, but it was judged to possess mere formal and peripheral significance, if not to be an actual burden to Jesus, and thus in fact it was largely discounted. The later criticism of the present century has, on the whole, been more consistently sceptical or agnostic on the subject of the historicity of the messianic consciousness, and hence has also gone even further than the old liberalism in denying a place to Jesus within the gospel of the kingdom. Perhaps the extreme of scepticism in this regard is found in Bultmann's declarations to the effect that, while he himself is confident that Jesus Christ was an actual historical person and was the herald of a distinctive message, his own indifference to 'Christ according to the flesh' is such that he would be content, if any one should insist upon it, to place the name Jesus in quotation marks as an abbreviated designation of the historical phenomenon.[1]

We should be going far afield from our present purpose if we undertook here an analysis and critique of modern opinion which, proceeding from the dogmatic judgment that the Christ of the Gospels cannot be the Jesus of history, seeks to recover a supposedly earlier gospel, which inevitably is discovered to be a Christless gospel. But we may profitably take account of the critical exegesis in our effort to discover exactly what the Gospels themselves have to say.

Now when we consider the impact of Jesus' preaching and appearance at Nazareth, we cannot doubt that the Lucan narrative establishes an intimate and indissoluble connection between the activity of Jesus Himself and the coming of the kingdom. When Jesus declares, 'Today this scripture is fulfilled in your hearing,' He signifies that the promised manifestation of the new order was realized, at least incipiently, and the only evidence that this was so is that Jesus Himself was proclaiming it to be a fact.

Having considered the passage from Isaiah from the viewpoint of its testimony to the coming kingdom, it is vital to observe that it also contains a distinctly personal note, and it is the personal aspect of the quotation that forms the immediate background for an evaluation of Jesus' own claims. The Scripture reading began:

[1] See *Die Forschung der synoptischen Evangelien*, 2te Aufl., 1930, pp. 32 f.; *Jesus*, pp. 12 ff.; 'Zur Frage der Christologie,' in *Glauben und Verstehen*, 1933, pp. 100 f. Cf. my discussion in WThJ, I, pp. 29 f.

'The Spirit of the Lord is *upon Me*, because He hath anointed *Me* to preach good tidings to the poor; He hath sent *Me* to proclaim release to the captives.'

The fascinating but rather intricate question as to the exact place of Isaiah's reflections upon the anointed one in chapter lxi within the larger context of his messianic prophecies in general and his portrayal of the Servant of the Lord in particular need not be evaluated here, for the decisions reached as to the Lucan passage are not dependent upon reaching certainty regarding it. The anointed prophet who speaks in Is. lxi is not specifically identified as 'the Servant of the Lord' or as 'the Anointed of the Lord.' Yet it is surely not insignificant that the functions ascribed to him have been associated in large part with the ministry of the Servant of the Lord. And though the language used in Is. lxi need not be restricted to the Messiah, the fact is that the one who appears there is described as one who is chosen and appointed, and evidently qualified, to discharge a pre-eminent function in relation to the coming kingdom, and thus the language is supremely appropriate as a reference to the Messiah. Moreover, even if the flexibility of the prophetic language in general would prohibit taking the words as an exclusive prophecy of Jesus Christ, there could be no doubt that Jesus himself, according to Luke, refers the personal aspect of the prophecy directly to Himself, and that within the context of the Gospel as a whole the one upon whom the Spirit came is regarded as none other than the Messiah.[1] In brief, therefore, Jesus' quotation of Isaiah, and His declaration concerning its fulfilment, thrust His own person forward as an integral aspect of His message, and intimated the pre-eminence of His claim to declare the word and will of God.

In spite of the unmistakable personal note which Luke strikes here, however, it is highly necessary to avoid exaggerating the positiveness of the disclosure.[2] There are significant silences and

[1] See Lk. vii. 19 ff. (Mt. xi. 3 ff.).

[2] R. H. Lightfoot, *History and Interpretation*, p. 202, regards the personal note in Luke as at variance with Mark, 'our primary authority for the earliest teaching of Jesus.' This teaching, he says, 'seems to have in view a general call to repentance, in view of the great nearness of the kingdom of God,' and adds, 'We may say with some confidence that in its first stages it contained no reference to Himself.' Is Lightfoot prepared to argue that Mark ii. 10, 28, for example, constitute a later stratum of development in Jesus' teaching, or are such features rejected outright as due to the supposed dogmatizing of the early Church?

a marked note of reserve that may not be overlooked. Though Luke no doubt regarded Jesus as the Christ and as the Servant of the Lord, he does not represent Jesus as making such claims at this point in any direct fashion. The words, 'The Spirit of the Lord is upon Me,' are a quotation from Scripture, and are not in themselves, therefore, a personal avowal. It is only the declaration, 'This day is this scripture fulfilled in your hearing,' which immediately, but still somewhat obliquely, brings intimations of His personal implication and participation in the fulfilment of the divine plan.

Moreover, the reserve with which the messianic claim is being asserted at Nazareth is unmistakably evident from the absorption with the *prophetic* function, for the prophetic activity serves less compellingly than the kingly and priestly functions to establish the indispensability of the ministry of the Christ to the establishment of the kingdom. The scriptural quotation treats only of proclamation, not of the actual defeat of the enemies of God nor of the removing of the burdens of the oppressed. And in the proverb which He refers to Himself He implies that it is *as a prophet* that He is unacceptable in His own home. There is far from being a manifestation of the fullness of messianic prerogative. It appears, accordingly, that it is only with considerable exaggeration that one could characterize the Nazareth story as programmatic for the entire Gospel or as containing the leading motifs of the Gospel.

How shall one, then, evaluate the place of this narrative within the broader structure of Luke's portrayal of Christ's ministry? Perhaps there is more than one answer to this inquiry. It may be that Luke intends to illustrate the *earlier* preaching of Jesus, and, on the background of the reserve with which the Messiahship was disclosed at Nazareth, to point to the fact that it was revealed to men with greater and greater fullness and explicitness as the historical career unfolded. But, at any rate, a more conspicuous characteristic of the incident claims our attention. More basic than the factor of development from the partial and simple to the more comprehensive and complex is the observation that the evangelist regards the course of things at Nazareth as being *quite untypical* of the Galilean ministry as a whole.

Jesus was unwilling to perform cures at Nazareth and thus He does not disclose *by deed* that the kingdom of God had come upon them. At other points in the ministry of Jesus there is also considerable reserve with regard to the performance of miracles: there are injunctions to silence concerning cures that had been effected; there are withdrawals from scenes of healing activity. But nowhere, it seems, does He so deliberately refrain from performing miracles as here at Nazareth. The discourse of Jesus, which has already been considered in an earlier connection in some detail, shows that His fellow townsmen expected and desired a display of power, but that Jesus was unwilling to conform to their expectations. Here clearly He would not appear as a miracle worker, a thaumaturgist.

The point made most pervasively and emphatically by the entire narrative is missed if what happened at Nazareth is conceived of as disclosing a leading motif of Luke's Gospel as a whole. The opening words of Jesus may be regarded as generally indicative of the contents of His message, but the further actions and reactions of Jesus and His hearers are underscored as being completely unrepresentative. Although the working of miracles could easily lead to misunderstanding of the purposes of Jesus, He acknowledges that He has performed them at Capernaum, and He takes it for granted that these acts would have been widely reported, or at least that His fame would have reached His own city. There is no suggestion that Jesus wishes to conceal the fact that He had carried on a healing ministry elsewhere. But what He refuses emphatically to do is to perform such miracles *in His own patris*.

That the entire emphasis of the narrative falls upon what would not occur at Nazareth, but could be expected to happen elsewhere, is borne out further, in my judgment, by the concluding words of Jesus. Following the quotation of the proverb, 'No prophet is acceptable in his own country,' Jesus says:

> 'But of a truth I say unto you, There were many widows in Israel in the days of Elijah, when the heaven was shut up three years and six months, when there came a great famine over all the land; and unto none of them was Elijah sent, but only to Zarephath, in the land of Sidon, unto a woman that was a widow. And there were many lepers in Israel in the time of

Elisha the prophet; and none of them was cleansed, but only Naaman the Syrian' (Lk. iv. 25-27).

It is popular today to regard these words as pointing to another motif in Luke's Gospel, namely, the feature of universalism including specifically the Gentile mission. Thus Creed says:

> 'Jesus is represented as appealing to the precedents of Elijah and Elisha who worked miracles for aliens rather than for their own country-men, to explain why His own miracles performed at Capernaum had not been repeated at Nazareth . . . the incidents cited from the careers of Elijah and Elisha provide good precedents for a mission to the Gentiles—and this no doubt was their real significance to the evangelist—but the implied analogy between the inhabitants of Capernaum and the heathen widow of Sarepta and Naaman is too remote to be original.
>
> 'The narrative must not be pressed . . . Its real function is to introduce the main *motifs* which are to recur throughout the Gospel and the Acts . . . The rejection by Nazareth foreshadows the rejection by the Jewish people and the subsequent universal mission of the Church.'[1]

Once again the insistence that Luke is freely shaping the tradition so as to introduce the leading motifs of the Gospel at the very beginning results in a forced and unnatural interpretation, which Creed himself is unwilling to attribute to Jesus on the ground that the analogy is 'too remote to be original.' A great deal is indeed being read into the allusions to the experience of the widow of Zarephath and Naaman when they are interpreted as intimations of the Gentile mission; if Luke were constructing a narrative with a view to centring attention upon the universalism of the gospel, would he not have done so with far greater explicitness and clarity? This view of Creed involves the judgment that Luke has introduced this motif in a very abrupt and awkward manner, for there has been nothing to suggest universalism in anything that precedes. Had that been Luke's intent it would have been easy for him, for example, to represent Jesus as including in the Scripture lesson intimations as to the dawn of light for the Gentiles. One must conclude, therefore, that the view that Luke

[1] Op. cit., p. 66; cf. Lightfoot, op. cit., p. 198.

is thrusting the motif of universalism into the foreground of his Gospel, regardless of the violence which is done to the tradition, is at the serious disadvantage of being both exceedingly abrupt and pitifully tenuous. If an interpretation not beset by these objections is available, it will have much to recommend it.

And exactly such an understanding of our Lord's references to the widow and to Naaman, perfectly prepared for in the preceding context and not taking us far afield, is at hand. Do not these allusions serve admirably to illustrate and establish the truth of the proverb that a prophet is not acceptable in his own country, which has been quoted because of its pertinence to the fact that Jesus had been rejected in His home city? Do not the references to the favour shown to a Sidonian and to a Syrian fulfil their purpose in expressing the thought that the power and grace of God had been manifested in unexpected places, not in the home of Elijah or of Elisha but rather beyond the area where, according to human expectations, their ministry would have made its impact? Sidon and Syria are contrasted with Israel solely to illustrate the fact that in Capernaum and in the remoter regions of Galilee Jesus had performed miracles and had been received favourably, whereas in the very place where He had been brought up He was unwilling to manifest His power and was rejected. The supposed allusion to the Gentile mission is accordingly left without basis in fact. The reactions of scepticism, wrath and murderous hate disclosed at Nazareth are viewed as exceptional and isolated within the developing Galilean ministry.

Although Luke presents the rejection at Nazareth as quite exceptional, it is nevertheless extraordinarily arresting that this discordant note is struck at the very beginning of his narrative of our Lord's public ministry. Its prominent position exhibits forcefully and even spectacularly the fact that Jesus would not win universal acclaim. And one may also recognize that, in the context of the entire Gospel, with the overpowering accent which it, in common with the other Gospels, places upon the passion and death of Christ, the rejection at Nazareth serves to prepare the way for the understanding of the more encompassing rejection which lay ahead. As Simeon had said, the Child was set 'for the falling and rising up of many in Israel; and for a sign which is spoken against' (ii. 34).

The question why Jesus was rejected by His own townsmen remains. Although Matthew and Mark place the story much later, they too do not suggest that the conflict is to be explained in terms of a long period of developing tension. On the contrary, they explain the results simply in terms of unbelief. Mark declares that Jesus 'marvelled because of their unbelief' (Mk. vi. 6; cf. Mt. xiii. 58). Such unbelief might indeed have certain historical antecedents, but the impression is given that, in the last analysis, the men of Nazareth failed to believe on Him because of the hardness of their hearts.

Although Luke's narrative does not make specific mention of their unbelief, the thrust of his account does not create an impression contrary to that given by Matthew and Mark. Jesus detects a basic scepticism in their attitude. But in Luke there is in addition the suggestion of another factor which centres in the divine purposes and actions. Jesus appears to perceive that there was a certain inevitability that His own people at Nazareth would not receive Him, that a mysterious, divine plan rather than a pattern of human expectations was being followed.

Yet the men of Nazareth are fully accountable. The gospel was preached to them. Nor does the consideration that no miracles were done in their midst alter the situation; to the extent that their being performed entered into the fulfilment of the good tidings it should have sufficed that miracles had been done in Capernaum and that the report of their occurrence had reached Nazareth. Thus 'the thoughts of many hearts' are revealed at Nazareth, and Jesus Christ is disclosed to be a stone of stumbling and a rock of offence.

Nevertheless, the proclamation of the divine word of promise and fulfilment gives assurance that the stone thus rejected of men would become the head of the corner (Lk. xx. 17 f.)

CHAPTER V

THE GALILEAN MINISTRY AS A WHOLE

THE consideration of the preaching of Jesus at Nazareth has served to centre attention upon certain aspects of the structure of Luke's narration of the public ministry. Although such questions lack the relevancy of profound issues like those pertaining to the message of Jesus concerning the coming of the kingdom of God, they demand an answer from serious students of the New Testament. Conclusions regarding them bear pointedly upon one's final judgments as to the essential character of the Gospels. The freedom with which Luke, for example, arranges his record of the ministry of Jesus as he tells of the unique experiences at Nazareth before relating the more typical incidents of the Capernaum cycle underlines the fact that he is not a mere chronicler but writes as an evangelist. As an evangelist he can allow himself considerable flexibility in the ordering of his materials. Nevertheless, there is no evidence that he is taking liberty with or doing violence to the facts at this point. In presenting the developments in Nazareth and Capernaum as illustrations of the ministry of Jesus in Galilee, he may not fairly be charged with arbitrarily fashioning a new chronological framework to suit his purposes of edification.

In the remainder of the record of the Galilean ministry there are no problems competing in interest and difficulty with that which has been already discussed. And one might be tempted, therefore, to pass over the comparatively tedious questions of structure in the interest of expediting the evaluation of what may appear to be more basic matters. But this temptation must be resisted. One cannot scrutinize too painstakingly the most minute details of the Gospel record, or take too much time in comparing the several accounts. As a matter of fact the Galilean ministry as a whole presents many fascinating questions in detail. And the problem of structure emerges with special acuteness in the middle chapters of Luke (leaving on one side for the moment the resurrection narrative), so that with regard to the evangelist's methods and aims one requires all the discernment that can be attained from the advance consideration of the earlier record.[1] It is my purpose therefore to deal rather broadly with the Galilean ministry in this chapter.[2]

CORRESPONDENCE WITH MARK

As one proceeds with an examination of Luke's portrayal of the public ministry, one is struck especially with the extent of his agreement with Mark. Matthew also is in close correspondence with Mark in the latter part of the Gospel narratives, but Luke's agreement is far more comprehensive. Luke includes nearly all the incidents found in Mark, and in such pervasive agreement of order that even many scholars who have not adopted the two-document theory of Gospel origins, or one of its variations, have come to regard the direct dependence of Luke upon Mark as demonstrated. The agreement with Mark is all the more remarkable because of the distinctiveness of Luke at many other points, a fact which has been brought to light in the sections of Luke which have already been evaluated. Nor does what looks like the interpolation of non-Marcan materials at a number of points within the Marcan framework serve otherwise than to place in sharper relief the parallelism of the corresponding sections.

There are three Marcan 'blocks' in the Lucan structure: (1) iv. 31-44 (cf. Mk. i. 21-39); (2) v. 12–vi. 16 (cf. Mk. i. 40–iii. 19); (3) viii. 4–ix. 17 (cf. Mk. iii. 20–vi. 44). In addition to the distinctive Lucan narrative of the ministry at Nazareth, there are three departures from the Marcan outline. The first is the insertion between the first two 'blocks' of the very brief episode of the miraculous catch of fish (Lk. v. 1-11). Of considerably greater moment are the materials in Lk. vi. 17–viii. 3, which contain many features that can be paralleled in Matthew. And finally

[1] Urgency is added to this examination by the significant evaluation of the framework of the gospel history in K. L. Schmidt, *Der Rahmen der Geschichte Jesu*, 1919, and in *Formgeschichte* generally.

[2] Lk. iv. 14, clearly marks the *terminus a quo*. The *terminus ad quem* is less definite. At any rate, it seems most convenient to draw the line at a point just before the confession of Peter rather than later when Galilee is finally left behind. Though the situation in Luke is somewhat more complex than in the other synoptic Gospels, here, as well as in Matthew and Mark, there emerges in connection with Peter's confession an occupation with the great climax of the ministry in Jerusalem that sets the middle section apart from the earlier delineation of the ministry in Galilee. Accordingly, we shall be concerned here with Lk. iv. 14-ix. 17.

there is the observation of a different kind that Luke appears suddenly and sharply to leave off paralleling Mark following the third 'block,' and contains nothing corresponding to Mk. vi. 45–viii. 26. On the assumption that Luke used Mark there are therefore instances of borrowings from Mark but also of additions and omissions. A study of both these sections where Luke appears to be on his own and of the passages where he is dependent on Mark may be expected to illumine the question of his literary and historical method.

The agreement between Luke and Mark is perhaps most clearly exemplified in the first of the three parallel sections (iv. 31-44; Mk. i. 21-39; cf. Mt. viii. 14-17). Both relate in order Jesus' teaching in the synagogue in Capernaum, the astonishment because of His authority, the healing of a demoniac who was present and His resultant fame, His departure to the house of Simon where Simon's mother-in-law was healed of a fever, and the healing of many that evening. The accounts are also closely parallel in reporting next Jesus' retirement to a desert place and in relating in summary fashion a preaching ministry in the synagogues. Here there is certainly no lack of interest in the precise locality and time of the several incidents within this single cycle (cf. Lk. iv. 31, 38, 40, 42). On the other hand, neither Mark nor Luke indicates any concern to define more precisely the setting of this group of incidents within the broader framework of the Galilean ministry. As intimated above, the particular activity in Capernaum is evidently meant to illustrate the Galilean activity as a whole (cf. Lk. iv. 43).

There is, however, one interesting difference between Luke and Mark in this context. Whereas Mark concludes this section by describing in general terms Jesus' activity 'throughout all Galilee,' Luke, according to what appears to be the correct text, states that Jesus 'was preaching in the synagogues of *Judæa*' (Mk. i. 39; Lk. iv. 44; cf. Mt. iv. 23). It is true indeed that Tischendorf and some other modern editors accept the reading 'Galilee' rather than 'Judæa.' 'Galilee,' as a matter of fact, is found in Codex Bezae and the Latin versions, as well as in the mass of the cursives, and might seem to be required as the evident intention of the evangelist. However, the reading 'Judæa' is supported by powerful considerations. It is the text of the great uncials Aleph, B and L, of certain distinctive cursives, the Sinaitic Syriac, and the consensus of the Coptic versions. Moreover, the origin of the reading 'Galilee' is far easier to account for on the assumption that 'Judæa' is the original reading than, on the contrary assumption, to account for the origin of the reading 'Judæa.' The apparent incongruity of the reading 'Judæa' within the context of the Galilean ministry constitutes it as the harder reading. But is it actually intrinsically impossible? If Luke intended at this point suddenly to refer to a phase of activity in southern Palestine, he would be guilty of introducing confusion into his narrative. But the fact is, as a survey of Lucan usage easily demonstrates, that the designation 'Judæa' signifies 'the land of the Jews,' that is, Palestine as a whole.[1] There is, then, no contradiction or confusion in Luke. But there is the difference that at this point he does not confine the ministry of Jesus so strictly as Mark to the bounds of Galilee, but allows himself, in the midst of his narration of Jesus' ministry in Galilee, to take note of the broader sphere of His preaching. Luke is also interested in the specific location of Jesus' activity, but he appears to be somewhat less concerned than the others to mark off from the rest of His work a ministry confined to the north.

Lk. v. 1-11 interrupts the parallel course of the Lucan and Marcan narratives with the story of the marvellous draught of fishes, one of the six miracle stories peculiar to Luke.[2] But the

[1] Thus Herod is described as king of 'Judæa' in i. 5, and Galilee is specifically included within Judæa in xxiii. 5, and Acts x. 37. Cf. also vi. 17; vii. 17; Acts ii. 9.

There is no reason to suppose that the non-mention of Galilee is due to a dogmatic construction. It is noteworthy that R. H. Lightfoot is much more reserved in finding doctrinal implications in Luke's references to locality than in Mark's. He speaks of Galilee as having equal significance and worth with Samaria and Jerusalem, but maintains that the presentation of Jerusalem as the goal and the culminating scene of the Lord's activity 'rests not only on historical considerations but on the doctrinal conception that Jesus is primarily Messiah, the lawful King of Israel, who receives the throne of His father David, and will be King over the house of David for ever' (Lk. i. 32 f. *Locality and Doctrine*, p. 143; cf. pp. 134, 136, 137). Actually, of course, Lk. i. 33, says that He will reign over the house of *Jacob* for ever. As Messiah, the Son of David, He will therefore reign over the whole of Israel. Evidence is lacking, therefore, that the interest in Jerusalem expresses a messianic motif.

[2] The raising of the widow's son at Nain (vii. 11-17) is the only other one within the record of the Galilean ministry where thirteen of the total of twenty are found. Three peculiar to Luke are found in the middle section: the infirm woman

climax of the story is found in the word to Peter: 'Do not be afraid; henceforth you will be catching men' (verse 10 RSV). As regards the calling of the disciples, it may be recognized as having elements of correspondence with Mark's account of the call of the disciples from their nets to follow Jesus, especially in view of the summons: 'Come ye after me, and I will make you to become fishers of men' (Mk. i. 16–20; cf. Mt. iv. 18 ff.). Nevertheless, the stories are basically so divergent that few commentators take Luke's miracle story as a mere reconstruction of Mark's account. And even if Luke's story were an amplification of Mark's, no problem of chronological sequence would emerge, for Luke tells the story without establishing any connection with what precedes or what follows.

But the question whether there is an historical difficulty in Luke's story remains. This narrative is indeed the first to mention contact with Peter, James and John. But this is not to say that Luke views this incident as establishing the initial contact with the disciples. His entrance into Simon's boat presupposes acquaintance with him (v. 3); previously there has been a report of the healing of Peter's mother-in-law (iv. 38). And strictly speaking the story, unlike the accounts in Mark and Matthew, is not occupied with a summons to the three disciples. Here James and John figure only secondarily. Basically the story is concerned with a profound personal experience which Peter underwent as he came face to face with the supernatural, and through which he comes to acknowledge Jesus as transcendent Lord: 'Depart from me; for I am a sinful man, O Lord' (verse 8). There is, therefore, no difficulty in supposing that the call to become fishers of men was repeated for emphasis since Jesus had in view that they should leave *all things* and follow Him (verse 11).

The parallelism of Lk. v. 12–vi. 16 and Mark i. 40–iii. 19 (cf. Mt. ix. 18–xi. 30) is also pervasive, extending to the narratives of the healing of a leper and of a paralytic, the call of Levi and the controversy occasioned by Jesus' fellowship with publicans, the question about fasting, the dispute occasioned by the disciples' plucking of grain on the sabbath, and the healing of the withered hand.

(xiii. 10-17); the dropsical man (xiv. 1-6); the ten lepers (xvii. 11-19). The sixth Lucan miracle (the only miracle recorded in the section concerned with the ministry in Jerusalem) is the healing of the servant's ear (xxii. 51).

Only at the very end of these sections does a problem of arrangement emerge, for there seems to be a transposition of certain incidents. Whereas Mark first speaks of a great multitude of people gathering to listen to Jesus and of His healing activity, (iii. 7-12) and then reports the choice of the twelve (iii. 13-19), Luke recounts the latter immediately after the story of the healing of the withered hand (vi. 12-16) and only afterward speaks of the gathering of a large crowd (vi. 17-19). The difference here is, however, not one of mere transposition. For in distinction from Mark who reports the two incidents as isolated events, the healing activity being placed 'at the sea' and the call of the twelve 'on the mountain', Luke in reality omits the former incident and, having related the naming of the twelve apostles, tells of a gathering of crowds when, in the course of Jesus' descent, he came to 'a level place.' The crowd, he says, came to hear Jesus and to be healed of their diseases (vi. 17). He then speaks of Jesus' response to their desires, relating first briefly the healing activity and then more particularly Jesus' discourse. On the assumption that Luke is dependent on Mark, therefore, one might possibly maintain that Luke has omitted the contents of Mk. iii. 7-12 in view of his purpose to refer almost immediately to a similar situation. It is misleading, however, to regard this arrangement as a mere transposition in view of the distinctive contents of Lk. vi. 17-19 as the introduction to the discourse that follows.[1]

The correspondence of Lk. v. 12–vi. 16 and Mk. i. 40–iii. 19 is not restricted to the order of events. It extends also to the relative indifference to geographical and temporal setting. In this section, in contrast to the preceding one, there are few signs of a definite itinerary in Mark, and Luke shows even less interest in fixing the time and place of the incidents. No particular difference can be noted in the story of the leper, although Luke vaguely describes it as taking place 'in one of the cities' (v. 12). In the account of the healing of the paralytic, on the other hand, Luke omits any reference to the locality which Mark designates as Capernaum, and his temporal phrase 'on one of these days' is hardly more precise than Mark's 'after some days' (Lk. v. 17; Mk. ii. 1). In

[1] Huck, *Synopse*, and Cadbury, *Style and Literary Method of Luke*, p. 77, classify this as a transposition. Burton and Goodspeed's *Harmony* takes the position supported here.

reporting this incident, Luke seems to show a special interest in the wide geographical distribution of the effects of Jesus' ministry, for where Mark merely speaks of a concourse of many, Luke reports the gathering of Pharisees and scribes 'out of every village of Galilee and Judæa and Jerusalem' (v. 17). Nevertheless, it would be too bold to claim this as a Lucan tendency, and especially to charge that a severe strain is being put upon the Marcan framework,[1] for Mark only a little later, at a point that can hardly be regarded as marking a significant new stage in the expansion of Jesus' ministry, speaks even more comprehensively of the impact of His work. In Mk. iii. 7 f. we read:

> 'And Jesus with His disciples withdrew to the sea; and a great multitude from Galilee followed; and from Judæa, and from Jerusalem, and from Idumæa, and beyond Jordan, and about Tyre and Sidon, a great multitude, hearing what great things He did, came unto Him.'

Even in vi. 17 Luke does not include mention of Idumæa and the region beyond Jordan. Finally, as characteristic of Luke's topographical interest, we note that he says nothing concerning the place of toll from which Levi was called, although Mark has stated that it was 'by the seaside' (Lk. v. 27; Mk. ii. 13 f.). For the rest Luke and Mark are in close correspondence in this section.

DISCOURSES AND MIRACLES

Lk. vi. 17-19, as has been noticed, serves to introduce an extensive section not paralleled in Mark. The Marcan arrangement is not resumed again until Lk. viii. 4 is introduced. This section of 86 verses of non-Marcan materials is easily the longest within the narrative devoted to the Galilean ministry (the other two such sections together comprise only 26 verses). Though non-Marcan, in contrast to nearly all that has gone before, the section contains much that is not exclusive to Luke for at many points there is close agreement with gospel tradition reported by Matthew.

That Luke shares with Matthew the desire to report the message of Jesus much more fully than Mark has done appears especially from the sermon reported in Lk. vi. 20-49. The extent of its parallelism with Matthew's 'Sermon on the Mount'

[1] Thus Lightfoot, *Locality and Doctrine*, p. 134.

suggests the possibility that both evangelists are reporting the same discourse. There seem indeed to be no insuperable difficulties besetting this hypothesis. The location may well be the same: Luke does not designate it as the sermon of the 'plain' or 'field,' and the 'level place' mentioned in Lk. vi. 17 may well be located on the side of the mountain. Nor may the relative brevity of Luke's report or the differences in detail between the two be appealed to as decisive for a contrary view. The brevity of the reports, in Matthew as well as in Luke, distinctly allows for the judgment that both have made a selection from a discourse which, as originally spoken, would presumably have taken considerably more time than that required for the delivery of the Sermon on the Mount. Although one is not in a position to state positively what principles have guided such a selection, it is plausible that the different audiences the evangelists had in view affected the decision. Thus, for example, Luke, contemplating his distinctively Gentile audience, may have decided to omit the antitheses of Mt. v.

On the other hand, the elements of agreement and difference in the two discourses are congruous with the view that Luke is reporting a discourse delivered on another occasion. Quite irrespective of one's judgment as to the precise length of the ministry of Jesus, there can be no doubt that it was widespread, that His teaching and preaching must have been repeated in similar form again and again, and that the gospel tradition preserves for us only a small segment of the total. Nor may one assume that Luke's knowledge of the tradition was confined to meagre literary sources. The details regarding the transmission of the gospel tradition are not sufficiently well known to permit a dogmatic judgment on questions of this kind.[1]

In the remaining paragraphs of the section under consideration, there are other substantial agreements with Matthew in the choice of incidents, but also certain narratives peculiar to Luke. Following the discourse of Lk. vi. 20-49, two miracles are reported, the first common to Matthew, and the second found only in Luke. These are the healing of the centurion's servant at Capernaum (vii. 1-10; Mt. viii. 5-13), and the raising of the widow's son at Nain

[1] On the entire question see especially Plummer, pp. 176 f.; Greijdanus, KNT, pp. 282 ff.

(vii. 11-17). These are followed with incidents where the teaching element is prominent, the first again finding its counterpart in Matthew and the second likewise being peculiar to Luke. The materials parallel with Matthaean data are the closely connected group consisting of the impatient inquiry of the Baptist concerning Christ and the testimony of Jesus concerning John (vii. 18-35; Mt. xi. 2-19); the story distinctive of Luke concerns the anointing in the house of Simon the Pharisee (vii. 36-50). The whole is rounded off with a summary statement of a ministry of preaching and healing which took place 'soon afterwards,' and in which certain women ministered to them (viii. 1-3; cf. xv. 41; Mt. xxvii. 55).

The arrangement of these materials suggests that logical considerations rather than topographical interests or literary influences have dictated their order. Though there are some references to time and place, it is clear that Luke does not place the incidents within the framework of an itinerary. Capernaum and Nain are mentioned as the location of the first two incidents, but there is nothing to suggest that a circuit of the cities of Galilee is in view. The interest in the narrative of the healing of the centurion's servant appears to be less in its connection with Capernaum than in the fact that such faith as the centurion manifested had not been found 'in Israel.' The action at Nain is linked temporally with the preceding context in a general way, however, for Lk. vii. 11 states that it occurred 'soon afterwards.'[1] Still another feature which indicates that this event is not presented as a quite isolated instance of miraculous activity is that Luke closes the account by indicating that the profound impression of the presence of the power of God created by the miracle was by no means confined to that city. Its effects comprehended 'the whole of Judæa' and even the areas beyond the land of the Jews (vii. 16 f.).

The inquiry of the Baptist is introduced without reference to

[1] Some ancient MSS., perhaps in the interest of a more specific reference, through the change of but a single letter, set the time as 'the next day'. This reading of TR and AV is also supported by Huck. The external evidence does not submit a clear pattern, for the TR also has the support of Aleph, C D W, some Old Latin MSS., and the Bohairic Coptic, whereas the other reading is supported by A B L Theta, certain MSS. of the Old Latin, the Sahidic Coptic, and the Sinaitic Syriac. 'Soon afterwards' seems to conform to the Lucan pattern. Cf. viii. 1.

time or place (vii. 18 ff.). It does indeed follow upon a report of John's disciple to John concerning 'all these things' (vii. 18), but this appears to have in view the total impression of the activity of Jesus rather than just the miracle at Nain. The logical progression from miracle activity to teaching as to the meaning of Jesus' mission reappears in Lk. vii. 21, 22, for further healing acts 'in that hour' become the background for Jesus' reply to John concerning His works. Similarly, there is no indication as to exactly when and where the anointing of Jesus in the house of Simon took place. It is introduced quite casually with the words: 'And one of the Pharisees desired him that he would eat with him' (vii. 36). But this Lucan story, occupied as it largely is with the exposure of Pharisaic lack of genuine love, has perhaps been suggested by the previous reflection upon the unbelief and hostility of the Pharisees (cf. vii. 30 ff.). The summary statement concerning the tour through 'cities and villages' which took place 'soon afterwards' presumably has the cities and villages of Galilee in view, but it is of interest that no specific mention is made of this locality.

The final section of the Galilean ministry where Luke closely follows the same order as Mark comprises Lk. viii. 4–ix. 17 (cf. Mk. iii. 20–vi. 44). Within this section, however, there are a number of departures from the Marcan order which require examination and which must be explained. The differences are as follows: (1) Luke does not include the parabolic discourses of Mk. iii. 23-30, although at later points he introduces materials that correspond more or less closely (cf. Lk. xi. 14-23, xii. 10). (2) Luke records the narrative concerning true kindred after the parabolic discourses, whereas Mark puts it before (Lk. viii. 19-21; Mk. iii. 31-35). (3) Luke 'omits' certain parables and comment on this teaching, although he includes one of these parables at a later point (Mk. iv. 26-34; cf. Lk. xiii. 18-19). (4) He further omits the account of the rejection at Nazareth as found in Mk. vi, but this, as intimated above, must be evaluated in connection with his distinctive narrative of Jesus' preaching and reception there. (5) He omits the story of the death of the Baptist which, as noted above, is explained by his inclusion of the imprisonment of John within the section devoted to the Baptist's ministry (Mk. vi. 17-29; Lk. iii. 19, 20).

While these divergences of order, apart from the story of the reception at Nazareth, do not pose any serious problems, they nevertheless are significant for our understanding of Luke's method. In the first place, he is frequently more concise than Mark. Perhaps this is simply a matter of style. But another factor may be that Luke felt the need of conserving space for the treatment of other matters, and especially for the great middle section. In the second place, in considering those instances where discourses of Jesus are omitted here apparently because they find a place in a later phase of the ministry, one should avoid the dogmatic conclusion that Luke has simply transferred the setting of these discourses without regard for their original historical occasion. Such a conclusion would indeed be demanded if it could be proved that Jesus never repeated Himself in His preaching and teaching and that Luke could not have had access to any tradition independent of Mark. Both of these judgments would involve an unrealistic conception of the transmission of the gospel before it was committed to writing in the Gospels. As Burton Scott Easton says, 'We must think of hundreds of instructions delivered in dozens of places. So there must have been an almost infinite repetition of material.' He further observes that, while many of the parables and sayings would have been repeated in the same form, other saying and parables would have received different form and different grouping on different occasions.[1]

Finally, bearing in mind the matter with which this chapter is chiefly concerned, and which is of the most fundamental importance as one considers variations of order in the Gospels, we observe that the differences in order of the various incidents require no special explanation if only Luke's evident method is kept in view. In this section, no less than in those previously examined, Luke shows even less concern than Mark to fix the place and time of the several events. Whereas Matthew and Mark introduce the parabolic discourses by reporting that the crowd at the seaside compelled Jesus to sit in a boat, Luke merely reports the presence of a crowd after referring in general terms to a journey 'through cities and villages' which came to pass 'soon afterwards' (Lk. viii. 1, 4; Mt. xiii. 1 f.; Mk. iv. 1f). Mark opens the story of the storm at sea with the precise temporal reference 'on that day when even

[1] *The Gospel before the Gospels*, 1928, p. 39; cf. pp. 122 f.

was come,' but Luke merely says that it came to pass 'on one of those days' (Mk. iv. 35; Lk. viii. 22). In the other narratives of this group Luke closely agrees with Mark in the presence or absence of geographical and chronological details.

RETIREMENT TO BETHSAIDA

In the final story in this section, however—the story of the feeding of the five thousand—Luke supplies a specific geographical reference not found in the other Gospels. He mentions in ix. 10 a retirement 'to a city called Bethsaida.' If the other evangelists were merely silent on this particular, no weighty problem would present itself. As a matter of fact, however, a complication arises because the reference to Bethsaida is not so distinctively Lucan as a comparison of the accounts of this miracle might suggest. For in the very next section, in reporting the miracle of Jesus' walking on the sea (which is not found in Luke), Mark likewise refers to a journey by boat towards Bethsaida (Mk. vi. 45). It may appear then that Luke gets Jesus to Bethsaida considerably before Mark does.

Before proceeding to a clarification of this problem, it is necessary to deal with two preliminary points which bear upon the interpretation of the Lucan narrative, one which concerns the motive for referring to Bethsaida at this juncture, and the second dealing with the consistency of Luke's own account with itself.

Is there an adequate explanation of the reference to Bethsaida at this point in Luke? Or is the evangelist open to the charge that he has merely anticipated the Marcan reference to Bethsaida because he plans to omit that Marcan section and must prepare for Lk. x. 13, which presupposes an activity in Bethsaida? Easton, for example, supports the latter theory. He says:

> 'The interval between the departure of the Twelve and their return is filled up by verses 7-9. No other connection appears to exist and, in particular, nothing here in Luke suggests that Christ went to Bethsaida to avoid Herod. Bethsaida, as a matter of fact, lay outside of Galilee, just across Jordan, but Luke does not indicate this in any way and his readers would not have known it. So in Luke the only apparent motive for Christ's withdrawal is a search for quiet.

> 'Such a geographical reference is contrary to Luke's usual practice, and it can be explained only as a preparation for x. 13. The name is taken from Mk. vi. 45, proving that Luke's copy of Mark did not contain a lacuna after vi. 44; Mk. viii. 22 is too remote . . .'[1]

The appeal to Lk. x. 13 is not impressive, since Luke does not feel it necessary to prepare for the reference to Chorazin in the same verse. It is natural therefore to look for the motive in the immediate context. Now it is true, as Mark reports, that Jesus sought a period of rest (vi. 31); but the insertion of the account of Herod's sudden interest in Jesus, including specifically his desire to see Jesus, whose name stirred up uncomfortable reminiscences of his beheading of the Baptist (Lk. ix. 9), can hardly be intended for any other purpose than to throw light upon Jesus' own actions. When, therefore, in Lk. ix. 10 Luke says that Jesus withdrew apart privately into a city called Bethsaida, he would have indicated to readers for whom the other geographical references had meaning that Jesus had left the region under Herod's domain for that of Philip's, Bethsaida being on the north-east coast of the lake, just within the border of Philip's tetrarchy.

The second question relates to the self-consistency of Luke's own account. The evangelist is sometimes charged with handling his Marcan source so clumsily, because of his supposed anticipation of the Marcan reference to Bethsaida in vi. 45, that he left his own account of the miracle of the feeding of the 5,000 in self-contradiction. Creed, for example, declares that, whether 'village' or 'city' be read as the correct text in Lk. ix. 10, 'there appears to be an inconsistency between this verse and verse 12:' in the first instance he is said to be in a city or village; in the second the disciples and multitude are said to be 'in a desert place.' Creed adds that Luke's inconsistency is due to his modification of Mark, and that his 'introduction of Bethsaida at this point is probably a sign that he was acquainted with the Marcan material at the end of this paragraph.' Since the crowds were compelled to go to the villages and country round about for lodging and provisions, it appears improbable that they could have been

[1] *The Gospel according to St. Luke*, ad ix. 10, and p. 138. Cf. Schmidt, op. cit., pp. 189 f., 193.

thought of as being in a populated centre. The intrinsic difficulty would be removed if one could adopt the reading of the Textus Receptus, 'to a desert place belonging to the city of Bethsaida.' But this reading, and other similar readings with meagre support, evidently arose from a desire to overcome this very difficulty.[1] Still this is not sufficient reason for concluding that Luke would have contradicted himself so flagrantly within the compass of three verses. It is a basic canon of criticism that, particularly in the case of a conscientious writer, one must assume self-consistency until the contrary has been firmly established. In this case clearly one must avoid undue rigidity in the interpretation of terms. As Easton points out in his comment on this passage, ' "city" here can only mean "city state".' The usage in Lk. viii. 26, 27, 39 affords a good parallel, for there 'city' evidently has in view the *district* of the Gerasenes. If then, Luke had in mind to point out that Jesus retired to a place outside the borders of Galilee, which he designates rather generally as the district of Bethsaida, it was still possible for him, in describing the situation which occasioned the feeding of the multitude, to speak more precisely of the place as an isolated spot where no lodging or provisions were available.

The question of the harmony of Luke with Mark remains. How can both evangelists be accurate if one locates the arrival in the vicinity of Bethsaida after a journey which *preceded* the feeding of the five thousand (Lk. ix. 11-17) whereas the other tells of the command of the disciples to sail to Bethsaida *after the miracle* while he dismissed the multitude (Mk. vi. 45). Luke, as has been observed, seems to get Jesus to Bethsaida considerably before Mark does. In the older discussions a solution of the problem was often found in the conjecture, supposedly supported by Jn. i. 44 ('Philip was from Bethsaida, of the city of Andrew and Peter'), that there was another Bethsaida on the western side of the lake.[2] However, there does not appear to be any real foundation for this view.[3] Nevertheless, unless one prejudges the case by the assumption that Luke everywhere is characterized by a slavish dependence upon Mark, there is no adequate basis for the con-

[1] On the textual evidence, and some of the issues involved, cf. Streeter, op. cit., pp. 568 ff., and Creed ad ix. 10.

[2] So Alexander and Gould on Mark vi. 45.

[3] Cf. Dalman, *Orte und Wege Jesu*, p. 158.

clusion that Luke has arbitrarily anticipated the arrival in Bethsaida. Matthew and Mark tell of a sea voyage to the scene of the feeding of the multitude, and Luke adds the information that this place was in the general vicinity of Bethsaida (Mt. xiv. 13; Mk. vi. 32; Lk. ix. 10). Luke does not tell what happened next; from a comparison with the other Gospels it appears that he here breaks off the narrative rather sharply. Matthew and Mark, on the other hand, report a sea voyage of the disciples which took them away from the place where the multitude was gathered, a voyage which began without Jesus and which soon ran into a fearful storm during which Jesus came walking to them upon the water (Mt. xiv. 22 ff.; Mk. vi. 45 ff.). After the storm they landed in Gennesaret on the western side of the lake (Mt. xiv. 31; Mk. vi. 53). So far there is a perfectly harmonious and consistent representation, quite in keeping with Luke's intimation that the multitude was fed at a point in the vicinity of Bethsaida near the northern end of the lake.[1]

Does not, however, Mark's report in vi. 45, that Jesus 'constrained His disciples to enter into the boat, and to go before Him unto the other side to Bethsaida,' introduce a contradiction? Actually, of course, Mark does not say anything of a voyage to Bethsaida, but only of an injunction of Jesus that they sail to, or towards, Bethsaida. It appears from the narrative that the storm may have prevented their ever reaching this destination; in any case we learn that they crossed over and landed in Gennesaret.[2] The ultimate issue, then, is whether, at a point in the general vicinity of Bethsaida (as indicated by Lk. ix. 10), Jesus could have contemplated a voyage of His disciples to the other side to, or towards, Bethsaida (as Mark states in vi. 45).[3] Cognate language

[1] Matthew's account does not contain the Marcan reference to Bethsaida. If his narrative is read without relation to Mark, one would naturally get the impression that the desert place was quite far removed from the vicinity of Gennesaret on the western side of the lake. It agrees well therefore with Luke ix. 10 ff. in placing the scene in the vicinity of Bethsaida.

[2] W. C. Allen, *Mark* (1915) ad vi. 53, however, on the basis of the western text, which reads, 'And having crossed over *thence* to the land, they came to Gennesaret and moored,' construes this as beginning a new paragraph, thus allowing for an interval between the events of Mk. vi. 45-52, and those introduced by verse 53. It is presumed then that the disciples actually arrived in Bethsaida; later they again crossed the lake and went to the land of Gennesaret.

[3] *εἰς τὸ πέραν πρὸς βηθσαϊδάν.*

is used on an occasion by Josephus in reporting a voyage of less than four miles.[1] Moreover, the Marcan account is highly congruous with the viewpoint that only a short voyage is contemplated, for evidently there is the expectation, which was frustrated by the storm, that Jesus would join them on the shore (cf. vi. 45 ff.).[2] Accordingly, Mark may well imply what Luke states explicitly, that the retirement of Jesus at this time was to a district bordering the lake on the north, of which Bethsaida was the centre.

The question of the so-called 'great omission' in Luke, that is the question why Luke closely agrees with the Marcan order as far as vi. 44, and resumes again at viii. 27, but passes over the materials found in Mk. vi. 45–viii. 26, is primarily a question of synoptic criticism, and not one that bears in any direct way upon the distinctive witness of Luke. On the assumption that Luke was familiar with this passage, it would not follow that he would think of its non-insertion as a great omission, for his very considerable independence of Mark at other points indicates that he would not have regarded his own plan as largely dictated by Mark's narrative. Hence, no dogmatic reply may be given as to the reasons why Luke does not follow Mark at this point. His interest in brevity and conciseness at various points, together with his intention of dealing at considerable length with other phases of Jesus' ministry, notably in the middle section, may have been a leading factor. Evidently Luke judged that he had set forth the basic features of the Galilean ministry with sufficient fullness and clarity in his selection of incidents and teaching, and that in particular it was not essential to his purpose to report several additional acts of healing and a second story of a miraculous feeding of a multitude. Nothing that may fairly be charged with being at variance with Luke's perspective appears in this section. At most one might say that such materials as the denunciation of the Pharisees (vii. 1-23; cf. viii. 11-21) would have appeared

[1] *Life*, 59 (304). Cf. G. A. Smith, *Historical Geography of the Holy Land*, 1902, pp. 457 f. Josephus says that, from Tiberias, 'he embarked and crossed over to Tarichaeae' (ἐμβὰς εἰς τὰς ταριχαίας διεπεραιώθην).

[2] Rawlinson, ad Mk. vi. 47, observes that '*In the midst of the sea* may mean "half-way across," but does not necessarily mean more than "a good way out from the shore".'

relatively inappropriate in a Gospel designed for Gentile readers.[1]

From the consideration of the early chapters devoted to the public ministry of Jesus, in which the parallelism with Mark, and to a lesser extent with Matthew, is so pervasive that we encounter comparatively little exclusively Lucan materials, we turn to the major problem of the middle chapters of Luke where the evangelist seems largely to go his own way. It may appear, however, that even in this section there is basic agreement with the perspective of the other evangelists.

[1] For the entire question cf. especially Hawkins, *Oxford Studies in the Synoptic Problem*, pp. 61 ff., 67; Streeter, op. cit., pp. 172 ff.; Taylor, *Behind the Third Gospel*, pp. 138 ff., 188 ff.

CHAPTER VI

FROM GALILEE TO JERUSALEM

ONE of the most extraordinary features of the canonical Gospels is their extensive occupation with the passion and resurrection of our Lord. Small wonder that in telling of the career of Jesus Christ the evangelists should have rounded off their narratives with the report of the stupendous and awe-inspiring fact of His resurrection, for the resurrection belonged in their thought to the age to come, and it was surely deserving of climactic treatment that for Christ that age had dawned. But the concentration upon the theme of the death of Christ, especially in writings which otherwise bear so little the mark of tragedy and indeed end on the note of glorious triumph and vindication, is a different matter. If other characteristics of the narratives, such as those which introduce Jesus to men as the divine Anointed and portray the astounding effects of His words and deeds upon men, had not already disclosed that the evangelists were not biographers telling the story of an historical figure of heroic dimensions, that would become luminously plain when once due weight was given to their overpowering interest in the theme of the passion. With very little exaggeration one might say that the Gospels are passion Gospels—with only so much space given to other details as are considered essential to the intelligible introduction of Him who was to go to the cross.

This evaluation of the Gospels applies most pointedly to Mark since its introduction of Jesus, like its taking leave of Jesus following the crucifixion, is exceedingly abrupt and since Mark's report of the teaching of Jesus is relatively brief. Mark may be said, like Paul, to know nothing save Christ and Him crucified. But if the disposition of materials in Mark excludes its categorization as biographical literature, but rather demands the recognition of a new and quite distinctive literary form, which cannot be more aptly named than simply by the use of the term Gospel, the situation is not essentially changed when one considers the other three. They may tell more of Christ's origin, His person, His message and the issue of His life, but they all likewise may be said to be absorbed above all with the story of the march to the cross and the meaning of that overwhelming event.

My purpose in this and the following chapters is to consider the place occupied within Luke's Gospel by the witness to the death and resurrection of Jesus Christ. So far as the concentration upon these closely integrated themes is concerned, Luke can hardly be said to be following a pattern different from that of Mark. His narrative of the resurrection is far more extensive; his narrative of the passion (in the narrower sense of the story of the events commencing with Christ's final entrance into Jerusalem and concluding with the crucifixion and the burial) is slightly briefer (about ten per cent); when both are combined Luke's account is somewhat, but only a little, longer than Mark's. If there is a difference in emphasis, then, between Mark and Luke, it is only because the latter is far longer than the former, somewhat more than half as long again.

INTRODUCTION OF THE PASSION THEME

The consideration of the broad disposition of the Gospels, while in itself not insignificant, serves chiefly to introduce the evaluation of the contents of the several narratives, and it will be my concern in what follows to deal with certain of the most remarkable features of Luke's representation. Before that, however, it is well to consider other evidence pertinent to the principal theme which confronts the reader well in advance of the narration of the climacteric events in the closing chapters. In Matthew and Mark the passion motif is introduced conspicuously in close connection with the withdrawal from Galilee, and is again and again brought into the focus of attention in their accounts of the journey to Jerusalem. The same or similar materials are also present in Luke. But in reading Luke the impression is sometimes received that there is quite a different perspective. Instead of the brief accounts of the journey from Galilee to Jerusalem found in Matthew and Mark, we encounter in Luke a section approximately three times as long as the corresponding sections in the other two synoptics, which frequently is thought to be occupied with a quite distinctive phase of the public ministry. I have chiefly in mind, of course, the great central section of Luke variously called 'The Lucan Travel Narrative' or 'The Great Interpolation,' comprising Lk.

ix. 51–xviii. 14. Although the special problem presented to students of the Gospels by this Lucan feature has too many facets to allow for a thorough evaluation here, it may not be ignored in view of its decisive bearing upon one's conception of the Gospel as a whole. And greater justice will be done to this problem, and to our basic theme, if this section is contemplated in the somewhat broader context introduced by the confession of Peter (ix. 18 ff.), and concluding with the actual arrival in Jerusalem (xix. 45).

Following the lead of Matthew and Mark, then, one may begin with a consideration of the manner in which the Confession of Peter became the occasion of the initiation of a solemn proclamation of the coming passion on the part of Jesus. When, however, Luke is compared with the other synoptics, one may receive the impression that Luke is less concerned than the others to mark this development as a new stage in the ministry of Christ. For Luke gives no intimation whatsoever of a withdrawal from Galilee to Caesarea Philippi which in Matthew and Mark sets the scene for the climacteric developments to come. Instead, he introduces the cycle of events in the most unobtrusive manner possible in the words: 'And it came to pass, as He was praying apart, the disciples were with him, and He asked them, saying, Who do the multitudes say that I am?' (ix. 18). If this evangelist were constantly and minutely concerned with the geographical and chronological framework of the gospel history, it would be difficult to overcome the impression that the confession of Peter and the events associated intimately with it were not intended to indicate a transition in the progress of events. Since, however, as the study of the Gospel as a whole demonstrates, such was not his aim, no special stress may be placed here upon the absence of any mention of a withdrawal from Galilee.

In spite of the absence of this feature, however, Luke no less strikingly centres the reader's attention upon the course of things to come. A comparison of Lk. ix. 18–50 with the closely corresponding narratives in Mk. viii. 27–ix. 41 and Mt. xvi. 13–xviii. 5 shows, in truth, that Luke marks the presence of the passion motif fully as emphatically as the others. In the first place, Luke is most explicit in noting the intimate connection between Peter's acknowledgment of Jesus' messiahship and the coming passion and resurrection (ix. 22). Whereas Matthew and Mark allow one to infer that the acknowledgment of Jesus' messianic dignity and His command that He should not be made known provide the occasion of, and offer the explanation for, His solemn disclosure concerning the future programme of the Messiah (cf. Mt. xvi. 21; Mk. viii. 31), Luke alone explicitly joins these features:

> 'And Peter answering said, The Christ of God. But He charged them, and commanded them to tell this to no man; *saying*, The Son of Man must suffer many things, and be rejected of the elders and chief priests and scribes, and be killed, and the third day be raised up.' (Lk. ix. 20 ff.)

Evidently the official proclamation of the Christ had to await the consummation of the messianic death and resurrection.

Even more conspicuously does the passion motif appear in Luke's account of the transfiguration (ix. 28 ff.). The transfiguration as set forth in the other accounts likewise must be understood, not as an isolated disclosure of Jesus' exalted dignity, but as a manifestation of divine approval of the course of action upon which Jesus had entered.[1] But Luke adds the significant item that the topic of conversation between Moses and Elijah concerned 'His decease (or, 'departure') which He was about to accomplish at Jerusalem' (ix. 31). In spite, therefore, of the absence of any reference to a change of scene and activity in Lk. ix. 18 ff., Luke even more pointedly than the other evangelists demonstrates that a new cycle of events is under way, which must take Jesus to Jerusalem for the climax of His ministry. The close connection of the transfiguration with the preceding disclosures concerning the coming passion is confirmed by Luke's distinctive reference to the time that had elapsed: it was 'about eight days after these sayings,' says Luke, that Jesus 'took with Him Peter and John and James, and went up into the mountain to pray' (ix. 28). In a context where the chronological details are so meagre, this reference emphasizes the inner connection between the stupendous developments and the disclosures in this section. Why Luke says that the period was 'about eight days,' whereas Matthew and Mark speak of six days, has never been satisfactorily explained on the basis of the theories which regard Luke as slavishly dependent upon Mark. If Luke were trying to improve upon Mark, it is

[1] See WMMC, pp. 68 f., 237.

difficult to understand why he should have submitted an indefinite measure of time for a more precise one, especially since there is substantial agreement between the two expressions.[1] But even this measure of independence stresses the close connection between the passion and the transfiguration.

DISPOSITION OF THE MIDDLE CHAPTERS

When one turns from the comparison of the parallel sections to the extensive travel narrative of Lk. ix. 51–xviii. 14, one faces squarely the major question of Luke's historical method. The final decision on this matter is necessarily bound up with the positions taken on broader historical and literary questions, including the identity of the evangelist, his sources of information, and his trustworthiness. To enter fully upon their evaluation would take us beyond the scope of the present discussion, but some stock must be taken of the main problem as it bears upon the disposition of the Gospel.

According to the most consistent representatives of the two-document hypothesis (which at this point means those who regard the third evangelist as rather exclusively an editor of Mark and 'Q' who, therefore, where he departs from Mark and the reconstructed 'Q,' is hardly likely to be publishing solid historical tradition), this entire middle section is to be regarded as being, at least so far as its references to time and place are concerned, essentially a creation of the evangelist. Creed, for example, maintains that, although Luke purports to describe a direct journey through Samaria to Jerusalem, this is inconsistent with references to Jericho (xviii. 35; xix. 1) as well as with mention of thronging multitudes, sabbath day preachings, offended Pharisees, and reports of Herod's hostility, which are said to suggest the background of the Galilean ministry rather than a set journey through Samaria to Jerusalem. The supposed discrepancy between the contents of this section and the framework of the journey is to be explained, according to Creed, as a literary construction. Wishing to incorporate a large body of

[1] As Plummer says, ad loc., 'it looks as if he had not seen their expression.' Luke also notes the intimate connection of the events following the transfiguration, for he, alone of the evangelists, introduces the story of the healing of the youthful demoniac with the expression 'on the following day,' which perhaps implies that the transfiguration took place at night. Cf. Lk. ix. 37.

teaching from 'Q' and certain material associating Jesus with Samaria, and wishing to avoid disturbance of the essential framework of Mark, Luke has simply imposed the element of continuous narrative upon the materials he desired to present.[1]

A somewhat higher estimate of the historical character of Luke's central section comes to expression among the advocates of the Proto-Luke Theory which, in contrast to a view like Creed's, allows that Mark was a secondary rather than a primary source for the third evangelist. And since, furthermore, it is widely held that Luke himself constructed Proto-Luke on the basis of 'Q' and distinctive tradition to which he had access, the unique materials in Luke are not so readily set aside as due chiefly to his editorial operations. On this perspective, although Luke is still thought to have introduced some incidents that rightly belong in Galilee, and his account is judged to betray certain gaps in his information concerning this period, Luke's theory is thought to be more than a mere literary device.[2]

No definite preference is being indicated for either view. In my judgment the choice is by no means limited to these two possibilities. And in any case the decision must be sought by a testing of the data as a whole, not by the simple expedient of determining which of several theories credits Luke with greater trustworthiness. One may again recognize, however, that the latter theory represents a salutary emphasis not found in the former, namely, that it credits the evangelist with a considerable measure of independence from previous literary efforts, a point which the author makes with some force in the prologue, and which finds impressive confirmation from the testimony of Acts to the authorship of the double work. The brief summary of these two tendencies in synoptic criticism, which are in part opposed to each other, serves, however, to provide a background for a review of the data in Luke.

In this extensive middle section one rarely loses sight of Jerusalem as the final destination, where Jesus' decease was about to be 'accomplished.' The section begins with the solemn declaration that Jesus 'set His face' that is, reached the fixed determination, to

[1] Cf. Creed, op. cit., pp. 139 ff.; Schmidt, *Rahmen*, pp. 246 ff.

[2] Cf. Taylor, *Behind the Third Gospel*, pp. 234 ff. See also Streeter, op. cit., pp. 203 f.

go to Jerusalem when the days were well-nigh come that He should be received up (ix. 51).[1] He was received with hostility when he entered into a village of the Samaritans because it was known, perhaps from messengers who had gone ahead, that His destination was Jerusalem, the centre of the religious fellowship which was the object of their implacable hatred (ix. 52 f.). That He was journeying to Jerusalem is also stated in Lk. xiii. 22 (33 f.), xvii. 11, and xviii. 31; He reaches the vicinity of Jericho in xviii. 35 ff., approaches Jerusalem at xix. 28, sees the city at xix. 41, and enters into the temple at xix. 45. At a number of other points Jesus is described less definitely as being on a journey (cf. ix. 56 f., x. 1, 38, xiv. 25). Since, however, many incidents and discourses are introduced without reference to an itinerary or other connecting links, it is not legitimate to conclude that Luke represents Jesus as continuously en route to Jerusalem.[2]

A rather popular evaluation of the problem is that which conceives of Luke as setting the scene of this phase of Jesus' ministry in Peræa. The journeying in view is regarded as following the longer route through Peræa, often taken by pilgrims on their way to Jerusalem in order to avoid contacts with the hostile Samaritans. Thus Luke is thought to be setting forth in detail what Mark has stated summarily in x. 1, where reference is made to Jesus' coming 'to the borders of Judæa and beyond the Jordan.' Although such an approach offers a simple, and in some respects attractive, solution of the problem of harmonizing the Gospel accounts, it breaks down on the mention of Samaritan activity within this section. The reference to the entrance into a village of the Samaritans in Lk. ix. 52 indeed would not rule out the idea of a Peræan ministry, since it might be allowed that the hostility of the Samaritans, which erupted in the first village which was entered after crossing the border of Galilee, caused Jesus to take a longer route. But an insuperable obstacle is presented by Lk.

[1] This appears to mean, more precisely, that the period to be concluded by His 'assumption' was drawing to a close. On the verb, cf. the usage in Acts ii. 1; on the meaning of 'assumption', cf. Acts i. 1 where the ascension of Christ is plainly in view.

[2] For a classification of the materials, see Schmidt, op. cit., pp. 248 f. Plummer's idea that Luke narrates 'journeyings to Jerusalem' is accordingly not positively supported by the evidence. Lk. x. 38, may imply that Jesus was in the vicinity of Jerusalem, but this too is not directly established by the evidence in Luke. Cf. Ogg, op. cit., p. 24.

xvii. 11 which discloses that Jesus is not, even at this late point, beyond the Jordan, but still 'passing along the borders of Samaria and Galilee.' It appears, then, that it is plainly a misnomer to speak of this section as concerned with 'The Peræan Ministry.'

But if this phase of the ministry may not fairly be called Peræan, may it not be correct to regard it as Samaritan? This is the conclusion of R. H. Lightfoot who maintains that Luke presents in succession three theatres of activity: Galilee, Samaria and Judæa.[1] And Creed at least partially agrees, for he maintains that Luke represents Jesus as taking the most direct route to Jerusalem, through Samaria, but that, through the influence of Mark's itinerary, he introduces a discrepancy by telling of His journey through Jericho (xviii. 35; cf. Mk. x. 46). The pertinent data, however, do not justify the adoption of these conclusions. The two references to Samaria (ix. 52, xvii. 11) are quite insufficient to ground the judgment that Luke purposes to narrate a ministry to the Samaritans or even one confined to Samaria. The very silence of Luke is a weighty consideration. If he intended to describe a distinctly Samaritan phase of the ministry of Christ, is it not remarkable that he neglects so many opportunities to make that clear to his readers? He might easily, for example, have stated that he had Samaria in mind when he speaks in Lk. x. 1 of 'every city and place where He was about to come.'[2] But the most decisive consideration against these views is presented by the specific testimony of Lk. xvii. 11. If this passage referred only to Samaria, there would indeed be plausible support for the theory that the middle section of Luke is concerned with Samaria. The fact is, however, that this verse places Jesus and his followers as much within *Galilee* as within Samaria. The translation of the verse is somewhat difficult, as is suggested by the marginal reading of the Revised Version 'through the midst' for 'along the borders' in the text:

> 'And it came to pass, as they were on the way to Jerusalem, that he was passing along the borders of Samaria and Galilee.'

Actually, however, there can be little question that Luke places

[1] *Locality and Doctrine*, pp. 137 ff., 143; cf. Lohmeyer, *Galiläa und Jerusalem*, 1936, pp. 41, 42 f.

[2] Cf. also Lk. xiii. 22, where similar language is used.

Jesus on the frontier of Samaria and Galilee.[1] So far as the evidence in Luke goes, therefore, it is not safe to go beyond the conclusion that a ministry near the border of Samaria and Galilee is in view, a ministry which may well have taken Jesus into Samaria on several occasions besides the one mentioned in Lk. ix. 52 f., but which also may well have included several stops in cities and villages of Galilee.

But if Jesus remained so long near the southern border of Galilee, how is one to make intelligible the frequent references to a journeying to Jerusalem? Jesus is indeed often viewed as proceeding on His way to Jerusalem, but the explicit references to Samaria and Galilee (ix. 51, xvii. 11) are congruous with the evaluation that Jesus was journeying, evidently in rather leisurely fashion, making stops at various cities and towns near the border. The references to Jerusalem do not imply that He was determined to reach Jerusalem in the shortest possible time and by the most direct route: they serve not so much to mark the outward course of the journey as to call attention to the inner purpose of Jesus which centres in His determination to reach the goal of His 'decease' and of his 'assumption' (Lk. ix. 31, 51).

Luke indeed is so far from marking out the exact course of the journey that, in contrast to Mark and Matthew, he does not even note the arrival in Judæa. One might perhaps gather from the third announcement of the coming passion that Jerusalem is near (Lk. xviii. 31), but no specific confirmation is given until the arrival in the vicinity of Jericho is recorded in Lk. xviii. 35. Then, however, Luke provides considerable information concerning the ministry of Jesus. For in addition to the story of the healing of a blind man, he reports the distinctive narrative of Jesus and Zacchaeus and the parable of the ten pounds, spoken 'because he was near Jerusalem and they supposed that the kingdom of God was immediately to appear' (Lk. xix. 11).

JESUS' MESSAGE TO ANTIPAS

That the frequent mention of Jerusalem in this section is due not to a concern on Luke's part to mark the course of the journey to that city, but rather to disclose the inner conviction of Jesus that

[1] On the textual and exegetical questions, cf. especially Plummer and Creed. The RSV translates: 'He was passing along between Samaria and Galilee.'

the messianic task was unthinkable apart from the programme of suffering and death which awaited Him, is impressively corroborated by the episode reported only by Luke in which Jesus addresses Herod Antipas (xiii. 31–33):

> 'In that very hour there came certain Pharisees, saying to Him, Get thee out, and go hence: for Herod would fain kill thee. And He said unto them, Go and say to that fox, Behold, I cast out devils and perform cures today and tomorrow, and the third day I am perfected. Howbeit I must go on My way today and tomorrow and the day following; for it cannot be that a prophet perish out of Jerusalem.'

The message is so singular both as to its occasion and its content that it claims more than passing notice.

However unusual the situation, it is surely quite intelligible that Antipas should have expressed a desire to kill Jesus. Not that he had determined to arrest Jesus and put Him out of the way, for in that case he would have done more than talk. But he was acting quite in character in seeking to intimidate Jesus that He might leave his territory. For this Herod, though a wicked man who could be utterly ruthless to gain his own ends (as shown in his divorce of his own wife, his marriage with his brother's wife, his imprisonment of the Baptist, if not in his order to have him executed), seems to have acted chiefly out of fear. For besides the fears which developed out of his political insecurity (due to his rivalry with Philip, the changing moods of the people, and especially the necessity of pleasing a succession of emperors, his failure in which led ultimately in A.D. 39 to his banishment to Gaul), there were the fears of his bad conscience. Knowing that the Baptist was a holy and righteous man, he had feared to put him to death (Mk. vi. 20). Later, when reports of Jesus' activity reached his ears, his evil conscience produced the interpretation that John had risen from the dead and 'therefore do these powers work in him' (Mk. vi. 14; Mt. xiv. 1 f.). Only when Jesus was finally arrested, and Pilate sent Jesus to him, could the cowardly bully be more or less at ease. For, as Luke alone reports,

> 'When Herod saw Jesus, he was exceeding glad; for he was of a long time desirous to see Him, because he had heard

concerning Him; and he hoped to see some miracle done by Him. And he questioned him in many words; but He answered him nothing. And the chief priests and the scribes stood, vehemently accusing Him. And Herod with his soldiers set Him at nought, and mocked Him, and arraying Him in gorgeous apparel sent him back to Pilate. And Herod and Pilate became friends with each other that very day; for before they were at enmity between themselves.'

(Lk. xxiii. 8-12.)

Antipas, accordingly, was a man who was deeply disturbed by the presence and activity of Jesus within his realm, for Jesus was a threat to his own security and a disturber of his peace of mind. He was entirely capable of uttering murderous threats though he seemed to lack the courage to deal summarily with the situation.[1]

That the intimidating threat of Herod should have been conveyed to Jesus by the Pharisees is also quite singular but altogether credible. In view of the constant evidences of tension between them, the Pharisees can hardly be regarded as having suddenly become friends of Jesus. Moreover, Jesus does not thank them, but treats them as if they were agents of Herod, and sends them back to him as if to say that He recognized that they were virtually associated with Herod in wishing that He might be killed. In complete consistency with the testimony of the Gospels as a whole, they may be understood as urging Jesus to leave Galilee either to weaken His cause in Galilee or to secure the advantage of His presence in Judæa where their own hostile power could be marshalled more effectively against Him through the activity of the Jewish Sanhedrin.[2]

Consequently, at the very time that Jesus of set purpose was shaping His ministry in terms of its climax at Jerusalem, the hostile secular and religious forces combined to seek to hasten Him on His way. In that peculiar situation, if Jesus allowed His course of action to be interpreted as influenced in the slightest

[1] This narrative provides incidental confirmation of the conclusions reached with regard to Lk. xvii. 11, since Antipas ruled over Galilee and Peræa. Inasmuch as the Lucan testimony excludes Peræa, Luke is implying that Jesus was still in Galilee.

[2] See 'Who Crucified Jesus?' in WThJ, V. 2 (May, 1943), pp. 137 ff., a discussion of Zeitlin's book with that title.

degree by such pressure, there would have been an obscuring of the decisive consideration that He was to go to Jerusalem completely apart from any outward constraint, but only because He freely and sovereignly, as His Anointed, undertook to do so in submission to the will of God. Accordingly, the first portion of Jesus' reply to Herod takes the form of a calm defiance of his threat.

Characterizing Herod as 'that fox,' and displaying neither fear of nor respect for him, Jesus lays bare the subterfuge and craft which he was employing. He first invites Herod to consider His works, the works which must have been known to Herod, for they had led him to conjecture fearfully that John the Baptist had risen from the dead: 'Go and say to that fox, Behold I cast out demons and perform cures today and tomorrow.' These works, the more so because Herod was not prepared to deny their genuineness, should have led him to repentance and restrained him from his evil course of sinning against his conscience as he had done in the case of the Baptist. There may, therefore, have been in these words a rebuke which should have compelled Herod to recognize that Jesus had done nothing worthy of death. Their main impact lies, however, in a different direction. For Jesus is insisting particularly that *He has work to do and that, despite Herod's threats, His work will go on*, not only 'today' but 'tomorrow.' He will not bring His mission to an abrupt close or seek to flee from Herod's domain.

The sovereign self-assurance of Jesus expressed here is unintelligible apart from the recognition of His consciousness of messianic authority. His work is not done by Herod's leave. There is a compulsion that transcends political pressure and the constraint of expediency. One is reminded of the manner in which Jesus had previously centred attention upon His works as evidence of His messianic authority when the Baptist had inquired from prison whether he was the one that should come:

> 'Go and tell John the things which ye have seen and heard; the blind receive their sight, the lame walk, the lepers are cleansed, and the deaf hear, the dead are raised up, the poor have the good tidings preached to them' (Lk. vii. 22 f.; Mt. xi. 4 f.).

If Herod had had ears to hear, he would have acknowledged that He whom he would fain have killed had come with divine authority and power.

But besides the public activity, which Jesus says must go on, He also points to the consummation of His life when he adds, 'And on the third day I finish my course.'[1] The thought evidently is that there is assurance that He will reach the end, or goal, of His ministry. Though Herod would fain secure His death to bring a catastrophic end to His ministry, Jesus considers His death as a consummation which is to be reached at exactly the proper and determined time. To interpret the reference to the 'third' day literally of the interval before the death of Christ would place Luke in hopeless contradiction with himself in the rest of the Gospel. Moreover, since Jesus is evidently speaking figuratively in declaring that His work would go on 'today and tomorrow,' His further statement concerning the consummation of His ministry as finding place on the 'third' day may not be fairly forced into a precise chronological framework. This reference to future developments, in spite of its indefiniteness, nevertheless serves to express the thought that a definite, prescribed time is in view, which will not be abbreviated or modified by threats. But since the period is measured in terms of days, Jesus appears to be intimating that the consummation is not far distant. He will not arrive at His goal before the appointed time, but He is marching forward with firm and rapid pace to the end.[2]

The message of Jesus to Herod does not conclude, however, on

[1] The ARmg and RSV take the form as a middle, and translate as 'end my course' and 'finish my course' respectively. The RV has 'I am perfected.' The passive is somewhat less appropriate in the context, which stresses Jesus' *activity*. One is reminded of Hebrews ii. 10 (cf. v. 9, vii. 28) where Jesus is declared to be made perfect through sufferings. To read the distinctive teaching of Hebrews into this saying of Jesus is surely too bold. Moreover, in Hebrews the 'perfecting' is viewed as a process of extensive duration, while here it relates only to the climax on 'the third day.' The notion that Hebrews and this Lucan passage alike have in view the idea of 'bringing Christ to the full moral perfection of His humanity,' as Plummer says in dependence upon Westcott, misses the point that Hebrews has in view the qualification of Christ to be a sympathetic priest. The New Testament nowhere supports the conception of a moral evolution of Jesus to a state of perfection.

[2] There is no necessity of resorting to the hypothesis of primitive textual corruption, as Wellhausen does, if the language is not construed in an unnecessarily literal fashion. Creed appears to share Wellhausen's outlook.

the note that Christ quite sovereignly and freely, regardless of human hatred and intimidations, will accomplish His mission and Himself write '*telos*' as the last word. For there is another motif in the Gospel, that of the necessity of the submission of the Servant of the Lord to the divine will. This motif receives somewhat distinctive expression when Jesus adds, 'Nevertheless I must go on My way today and tomorrow and the day following; for it cannot be that a prophet perish out of Jerusalem.' The Pharisees had said, 'Get thee out and go hence,' and Jesus had uttered His defiance. But now He admits that He must go to Jerusalem. The departure which the Pharisees suggested and Herod evidently had in view will inevitably take place but because of a stronger necessity than that of the decree or whims of tyrants.

This procession to Jerusalem must take place 'today, and tomorrow and the day following' and thus, like the carrying forward of His work to the appointed goal, will take place in the immediate future. Coincident with the active discharge of His mission there will be a constant facing towards the city where His decease would be accomplished.[1]

Although, then, the necessity of Jesus' march to Jerusalem as expressed at this time appears to echo other solemn utterances of the divine necessity of the passion, a somewhat different direction appears to be given to the argument in the words, 'For it cannot be that a prophet perish out of Jerusalem.' These words introduce an historical consideration as requiring His death at Jerusalem: not the working of an inexorable divine purpose, but rather an ironical and paradoxical consideration which centres attention upon the strange workings of the sinful heart of man. Jerusalem, the Holy City, the city where Jesus comes to manifest His glory and authority, over which He now pours out His heart in tender yearning, once again would have to experience its infamous distinction of being a murderer of the prophets! Not Galilee or Peræa, the domain of Herod, but Jerusalem, where a Roman procurator sits in judgment and where the Jewish Sanhedrin convenes, would be the scene of His death. There is therefore no mitigation of

[1] If Luke's language in verse 33 were meant to be taken literally he would apparently contradict his use of similar language in verse 32, for in the former instance He reaches His end on the third day and in the latter He is still going to Jerusalem on the day following 'today and tomorrow.' In both expressions Jesus is employing concrete but figurative language.

human guilt, no sanction of the action of those who would put Him to death, but a pointing to the inevitability that human sin should conspicuously display its own perversity. But even this perversity is subservient to the fulfilment of the divine purpose which compelled Jesus, in submission to Him who had sent Him, to go up to Jerusalem.

The recognition that the passion was to be explained basically in terms of the fulfilment of the divine plan, and yet in its historical realization would also manifest the enormity of human sin and guilt, came to even sharper focus later on. For at the last supper, in calling attention to the presence of the betrayer at the table, Jesus declared that 'the Son of Man goeth as it hath been determined; but woe unto that man through whom He is betrayed!' (xxii. 22). And Peter on the Day of Pentecost, in proclaiming Jesus of Nazareth, said: 'Him, being delivered up by the determinate counsel and foreknowledge of God, ye by the hand of lawless men did crucify and slay' (Acts ii. 23; cf. iv. 27 f.). But this perspective upon the messianic programme has been present from the beginning of explicit reflection upon the passion. It was conspicuously present in the solemn declarations concerning the necessity that the Son of Man should suffer many things and be betrayed into the hands of men, which, as has been noted, were intimately associated with the confession of Peter (ix. 22; cf. ix. 44). And even more vividly was it reiterated in the declaration of Lk. xviii. 31 ff., reported as having been uttered shortly before the arrival at Jericho:

> 'And He took unto Him the twelve, and said unto them Behold, we go up to Jerusalem, and all the things that are written by the prophets shall be accomplished unto the Son of Man. For He shall be delivered up unto the Gentiles, and shall be mocked, and shamefully entreated, and spit upon; and they shall scourge and kill Him: and the third day He shall rise again.'

In these sayings there appears, perhaps as an undertone, the note that the manner in which men treated Jesus, who as the Son of Man should have been accorded divine honours, was a shocking disclosure of the utter wickedness of the human heart.[1]

[1] Cf. G. Vos, *The Self-Disclosure of Jesus*, 1926, pp. 238 f.

COMPARISON WITH MARK

The survey of the middle chapters of Luke provides a useful background for the consideration of the harmony of the Lucan narrative with the data of Mark. In an earlier connection brief mention was made of the common judgment that Luke's distinctive middle section is reporting a Peræan ministry, to which Mark is thought to allude in x. 1. Since, however, as Lk. xvii. 11 particularly shows, Jesus is still at a late point on the borders of Samaria and Galilee, this evangelist cannot be thinking in terms of a Peræan ministry. Harmonization cannot be achieved, therefore, by the simple expedient of fitting this section into the framework of Mk. x. 1.

Do the Lucan references to Samaria, however, conflict with the Marcan representation concerning the transition from Galilee to Judæa? That might appear to be the case if Mark, as is often supposed, implies that the journey from Galilee to Judæa followed a route through Peræa along the eastern side of the Jordan. Though Mk. x. 1 may, as Swete says, have in view 'a considerable journey,' there is nothing to suggest that the journey was wholly or largely through Peræa; the passage teaches only that in connection with the journey he *arrived* in Peræa. This remains true also on the widely accepted western reading, 'Judæa beyond the Jordan,'[1] although the received text, in mentioning Judæa before Peræa, would add to the difficulty of construing the reference as a *journey through* Peræa. Actually Mark tells us nothing concerning the route by which Jesus travelled from Galilee to the South.[2]

Burkitt is particularly ingenious in suggesting a harmonization at this point.[3] Jesus is allowed, following Luke, to have travelled through Samaria, and it is supposed, in view of the mention of James and John in Lk. ix. 54, that they alone accompanied Him. But Peter and some other disciples took the eastern route through Peræa. And Mk. x. 1 was written from the point of view of Peter's observations (upon which Mark was dependent): he observes Jesus arriving in 'Judæa beyond the Jordan,' that is, on the *western* side of the river. Then the Peræan ministry would vanish

[1] E.g., by Wellhausen, Burkitt, *Gospel History and Its Transmission*, 1906, p. 96; Branscomb (MC).

[2] Cf. Rawlinson, ad loc.

[3] Op. cit., pp. 96 f.

in thin air. This theory, however, apart from its generally conjectural character, is under the severe burden of its assumption that 'beyond the Jordan' might well be understood of the area west of the Jordan.

Since, accordingly, Mark is silent concerning the course of Jesus' journey from Galilee to southern Palestine, the problem of the framework of the Lucan narrative is greatly relieved. But the question remains whether, assuming that Mk. x. 1 does not give the setting for Luke's middle chapters, this Gospel does not afford other points of contact with Luke. As a matter of fact, Mark's account does not fall simply into two sharply distinct divisions, the one Galilean and the other Judæan, without a transition from the one to the other. Although Galilee is finally left behind only at the end of Mk. ix, *the actual withdrawal begins much earlier*. The turning point in the narrative is found in the departure to the regions of Caesarea Philippi (Mk. viii. 27). Nevertheless, afterwards we hear of Jesus' passing through Galilee (ix. 30) and of activity in Capernaum (ix. 33 ff.). Lk. ix. 18–50 closely parallels Mk. viii. 27–ix. 50, and though Luke does not state where these events took place, the contents of the section, as noted above, indicate fully as emphatically as the Marcan account that they form a significant part of the story of the way to the cross at Jerusalem. Lk. ix. 51 ff. then provides us not so much with an account of a new phase and locality of Jesus' ministry as with a supplement to the meagre account found in Mark of the new stage inaugurated by Jesus' solemn pronouncement of His coming passion and resurrection. The activity on the way through Galilee, which Mark explicitly mentions in ix. 30, and the ministry along the borders of Samaria and Galilee, referred to by Luke in xvii. 11, may accordingly be viewed as parts of a larger whole, namely, the ministry in Galilee and northern Samaria which was undertaken in connection with the Lord's approach to the climactic events at Jerusalem.

On the background of these observations, one may observe how baseless the charge is that Luke has introduced Galilean materials into a non-Galilean framework. We have observed that, strictly speaking, there is no exclusively non-Galilean framework within this section. Therefore there is no good reason for doubting that reports of the hostility of Herod Antipas may have reached

Jesus as he was passing along the borders of Samaria and Galilee (Lk. xiii. 31, xvii. 11). Nor, unless it can be proved that the journey to Jerusalem was a direct one, without any stops in the cities and villages along the way, is there any improbability in the statement that 'He was teaching in one of the *synagogues* on the sabbath (Lk. xiii. 10). It might possibly be surprising to find contact with the Pharisees in the heart of Samaria, but no difficulty is created by the references in Lk. xi. 37 and xiv. 1 if Jesus was still on the Galilean frontier. The 'throngs' referred to in Lk. xi. 29, xii. 1, and xiv. 25, provide a picture which admittedly agrees ill with the notion that Jesus, accompanied only by the inner circle of disciples and perhaps a few others, went post-haste towards Jerusalem. Mark's account indeed concentrates one's attention so exclusively upon the passion of Christ, and upon the intimate disclosures to and reactions of the disciples, that there is little consideration of anything else.[1] Nevertheless, for Mark too, Jesus is not isolated from the crowds: they are about Jesus after the descent from the Mount of Transfiguration (Mk. ix. 14), and again there are crowds present when He teaches in Judæa (x. 1).[2]

[1] Cf. WMMC, pp. 37 f., 44 ff., 80, 118.

[2] Besides the charge that Luke creates discrepancies by introducing various situations that are not congruous with the notion of a journey, there is the more general claim that many of the discourses have been transported arbitrarily from 'Q' into this new framework. On the question of the existence of 'Q,' it is worthwhile to consider the viewpoint of Ropes, *The Synoptic Gospels*, pp. 37, 93, and Enslin, *Christian Beginnings*, 1938, pp. 431 ff.

The likelihood that Jesus frequently repeated His teaching in substantially the same form has been noted above. There is no compelling reason, for example, why Jesus would not have repeated at some later time His defence against the Beelzebub charge (cf. Mt. xii. 22 ff.; Mk. iii. 20 ff.; Lk. xi. 14 ff.).

CHAPTER VII

DEATH AND RESURRECTION

IN view of all that has gone before, as the preceding chapter particularly recalls, Luke's record of what actually happened at Jerusalem does not appear anticlimactic. The story of the passion and death of Christ, as of His resurrection, is presented as the accomplishment of the divine purpose. And Jesus Himself is not merely passive in the developments leading to the goal. Since the knowledge of the divine will controls His thought of His mission, He actively and self-consciously labours to bring about the destined consummation. In these respects, in spite of the different disposition of the Lucan narrative of the public ministry, there is profound agreement with the perspectives of the other Gospels. And, speaking broadly, there is basic agreement also in the records of what actually took place after Jesus had entered Jerusalem. Nevertheless there are features of Luke's closing chapters that have been viewed in modern times as pointing to a strikingly independent testimony concerning the actual course of events and their meaning for the understanding of Christianity. Their evaluation will chiefly occupy our attention in this chapter. Questions relating to structure will not be neglected, but the principal concern will be the meaning of the events themselves as that is disclosed by the teaching of Jesus.

By common consent Luke does not provide any specific knowledge as to the duration of the ministry in Jerusalem. Mark, and to a somewhat lesser extent Matthew, provide a rather clearer picture of the events of the several days of the week following the entry into the city. But even Mark does not indicate precisely the transition from day to day after the second day of the week, and he cannot fairly be regarded as aiming to offer a complete outline of the events of each day.[1] Nevertheless, the general vagueness of Luke is in remarkable contrast to the explicitness of Mark at many points.

Whereas Mark is careful to delineate the progress of events on the first day after the entry into the city, Luke virtually

[1] Cf. WMMC, p. 35.

supplies only a summary of the activity of Jesus there (Lk. xix. 47 f.). It is of moment that he omits altogether any reference to the incident of the cursing of the fig tree, and describes the cleansing of the temple with the utmost brevity (xix. 45 f.). Since Luke does not even refer explicitly to Jesus' entry into the city, it is unwarranted to state, as Creed does,[1] that on His entry Jesus 'proceeds at once' to the temple and expels the traders (cf. xix. 45). The casting out of the traders obviously presupposes Jesus' presence in the city, and it is the first incident mentioned by Luke which does so, but so far as the evangelist's own language is concerned this event might have occurred some time after His arrival.

The summary character of Luke's account is observed especially in the references to His teaching daily in the temple. The extensive record of the teaching given in Lk. xx and xxi, and described as delivered 'on one of the days, as He was teaching the people in the temple, and preaching the gospel' (xx. 1) finds close parallels to the teaching recorded in Matthew and Mark. But it is evidently intended to illustrate Jesus' teaching during the last days in Jerusalem, for it is presented as a kind of parenthesis between the references in Lk. xix. 47 and xxi. 37 to His custom of teaching daily in the temple.

An even more telling proof of Luke's relative lack of concern for a precise chronological outline of the events immediately preceding the crucifixion is disclosed by the manner in which the passion story is introduced. Whereas Matthew and Mark both begin with the intimation that the feast of the passover and of the unleavened bread was 'two days' away, Luke is content merely to state that it 'drew nigh' (Lk. xxii. 1; cf. Mt. xxvi. 2; Mk. xiv. 1). Omitting the anointing at Bethany, Luke centres attention upon the manner in which Judas, through Satanic inspiration, solved the problem confronting the Jewish rulers by promising to betray Jesus in the absence of the multitude (Lk. xxii. 2-6). Nevertheless, Luke as explicitly as the other Gospels associates the final developments with the celebration of the feast.

R. H. Lightfoot, in connection with his theory that, because of Luke's conception of Jesus as the Messiah, the lawful king of Israel, Jerusalem is viewed as the goal and culminating scene of

[1] Op. cit., p. 239.

activity, argues that the indefiniteness of Luke in such passages as xx. 1 and xxii. 1 offers further proof of his theory since the ministry in Jerusalem, rather than being marked off as lasting less than a week, thus appears to be of 'indeterminate duration.'[1] Apart from other objections to which this theory is subject, it seems particularly far-fetched to appeal to the indefiniteness of the duration of the activity of Jesus in Jerusalem in view of the accumulation of evidence that throughout the Gospel Luke again and again displays a remarkable lack of interest in chronological details.

So far as the rest of the passion narrative is concerned, no acute problems of order and locality present themselves. Luke continues at various points to be less definite than the other synoptics. The last supper begins 'when the hour was come,' not, as the other accounts state more explicitly, 'when it was evening' (Lk. xxii. 14; Mt. xxvi. 20; Mk. xiv. 17). Luke agrees with the others in stating that after the supper Jesus went unto the Mount of Olives (although Luke adds 'according to His custom'), but the particular place, identified by the other evangelists as Gethsemane, is left unnamed (Lk. xxii. 39 f.; cf. xxi. 37; Mt. xxvi. 30 ff.; Mk. xiv. 26 ff.). In the account of Jesus' appearance before Herod, reported only in Luke, the occasion is given as the charge before Pilate that Jesus 'stirreth up the people, teaching throughout all Judæa, and beginning from Galilee even unto this place' (Lk. xxiii. 5). But this provides no new information concerning the scope of the ministry in and around Jerusalem. Here as on other occasions 'Judæa' evidently means Palestine, the land of the Jews,[2] and 'this place' must be Jerusalem. The impact of the charge was to the effect that Jesus had created far more than a local disturbance, one that involved even Galilee.

THE MEANING OF CHRIST'S DEATH

There are two outstanding facts which are largely responsible for the judgment that Luke presents a perspective with regard to the significance of the death of Christ remarkably divergent from

[1] Cf. *Locality and Doctrine*, p. 141; cf. pp. 139 ff. I have shown that the theory is not well established so far as Mark is concerned. Cf. WMMC, pp. 38 ff. See also Chapter V, p. 96, note 1.

[2] See above, Ch. V, p. 96.

that found in the other synoptics. The first of these is that Luke fails to mention the 'ransom' saying reported in Mt. xx. 28 and Mk. x. 45, though in other respects he seems to parallel rather closely the contexts in which this saying is found. And the second fact is that Lk. xxii. 19b, 20, which contains the teaching that the cup is 'the new covenant in my blood which is poured out for you,' is judged by many textual critics today to be an interpolation.[1] Since it it these two passages which offer the most positive evidence that Jesus conceived of His death in terms of redemptive sacrifice, their omission from the Gospel according to Luke might point to a divergent view of the death of Christ or at least to a somewhat different emphasis with regard to it.

Evaluating these conclusions in relation to the other Lucan data, William Manson sums up the results by stating that 'on this view Luke's original text, following his Judæan source, made the Supper a prophecy of the Messianic banquet and a symbol of the disciples' fellowship with Christ, but not a representation of His sacrifice or a channel by which the results of that sacrifice are communicated.'[2] Recognizing the distinctiveness of the Lucan teaching in such terms, one might still allow that this evangelist supplements the other accounts rather than contradicts them. But in the modern situation one rarely encounters such a total judgment concerning the diversity of the witness of the records but rather an approach which is assured of basic discrepancies in the tradition and its interpretation and seeks to evaluate the origin of the various traditions within the development of Christianity as a whole. In this instance, that is characteristically true, for Luke is widely thought to display a distinctive theological point of view

[1] Hort's discussion in Westcott and Hort, *The New Testament in Greek*, 1882, Vol. II, Notes on Selected Readings, pp. 63 f., is the most basic argument for the view that Lk. xxii. 19b, 20 is an interpolation. The WH text, however, retains this passage as does RV, though the margin indicates that 'some ancient authorities omit' the passage. The RSV, on the other hand, omits the passage, and states in the margin that 'many ancient authorities add' it. The latter view is in keeping with the thrust of modern opinion, represented, for example, by Plummer, Easton, Creed, Wellhausen, B. Weiss, J. Weiss, Zahn and Klostermann. On the other side, cf. especially A. H. McNeile, *The Gospel according to St. Matthew*, 1915, pp. 385 f.; H. J. Holtzmann, *Die Synoptiker* (HC), 1901, p. 409; M. J. Lagrange, *Evangile selon Saint Luc*,[7] 1948, pp. 545 ff.; S. Greijdanus, *Lucas* (KNT), II, 1941, pp. 1045 ff.; *Lucas* (KV), II, 1941, pp. 217 f.

[2] Op. cit., p. 242.

and to present a quite independent conception of the origin of the Lord's Supper.[1]

The longer reading of Luke is omitted by Codex Bezae and certain manuscripts of the Old Latin versions, and thus belongs to a group of passages, mostly in the latter part of Luke's Gospel, which Hort grouped together as 'Western non-interpolations.' While recognizing the epochal significance of the work of Hort in the field of textual criticism, it is well to observe that the conclusions reached with regard to these passages as a group are not nearly so securely established as other basic features of that system, which themselves have been widely recognized as not allowing sufficiently for the weight of intrinsic considerations in individual cases. Streeter, for example, though still agreeing largely with the final conclusions of Westcott and Hort, challenged the propriety of setting as high a value upon any one form of text as they did, and in particular insisted that each of the so-called Western non-interpolations had to be judged on its own merits.[2] Accordingly, the fact of the absence of the words in question from D and certain allies cannot be regarded as particularly meaningful unless most weighty arguments compel the decision that the Western reading is the original.

It is precisely in the sphere of internal evidence, however, that many modern scholars judge that the case for the omission is particularly strong. In the first place, it is observed that the longer text involves the extraordinary situation that Luke has already in verse 17 referred to a dispensing of the cup, and thus the cup of verse 20, the passage in question, would be a second cup, and this reading is thought to be intrinsically difficult because of the resultant complexity of the representation of the course of events.[3] And in the second place, the origin of the longer reading is explained as due to the incorporation of language from 1 Cor.

[1] Creed, op. cit., p. 265, suggests that perhaps this element was 'not entirely congenial' to Luke himself; cf. pp. lxxi f., 261 ff. W. Manson, op. cit., p. xxv, regards the omission of the ransom saying as 'doubtless accidental'. He says further that 'theological interests were not paramount in the mind of Luke' and that 'his leaning is towards the emotional and practical aspects of religion, towards the elements of feeling and action.' Cf. also Cadbury, *Making*, pp. 280 f.

[2] Cf. op. cit., pp. 318, 330, 553 n. He does not express a final judgment on Lk. xxii. 19b, 20, though he seems sympathetic to Hort's conclusion. Cf. p. 553 n.

[3] Cf. Wellhausen, op. cit., p. 122: '. . . es kann doch nicht ein Mahl sofort auf das andere gesetzt und zweimal gegessen und getrunken werden.'

xi. 24, 25 at a time when the Lucan account would have been considered unsatisfactory as placing the cup before the breaking of the bread and defective because of the absence of the sacrificial feature. On the other hand, there is said to be no adequate explanation of the omission of the words on the understanding that the longer text was the original.[1]

These considerations do not, however, carry the weight, in my judgment, that is often assigned to them. In brief, my impression is that Luke's account, on the supposition that the longer text is Lucan, although containing some distinctive features, is characterized by intrinsic intelligibility and consistency. Such difficulties as appear are comparatively superficial and largely vanish in the light of exegetical and archæological investigation. On the other hand, the shorter text, though its divergences from the longer are commonly exaggerated, presents a substantially different conception of the Supper which is beset by insuperable exegetical and historical obstacles.

That the advocates of the shorter text generally stress the distinctiveness of Luke's representation of the Supper is hardly a matter of argument. This appears, for example, from the fact that the longer text is commonly regarded as the product of a process of harmonization which resulted when the need was felt of bringing Luke into line with records of the institution of the Supper. Creed, for example, holds that Luke did not think of the last Supper as 'a proclamation of the death of Christ according to a rite instituted by Jesus' but as simply one occasion among many of 'breaking bread.' Although Luke is thought not to reflect a primitive source, he is said to write 'in an age when Christian rites and institutions are still in a fluid state' and 'no fixed interpretation has become normative.'[2] There thus comes to expression a deep-seated scepticism with regard to the historicity of the

[1] Easton, op. cit., p. 321, makes the point that while the omission of verse 20 might be explained by its reference to a second cup, the omission of verse 19b would not thus be accounted for. R. Otto, *The Kingdom of God and the Son of Man*, n.d., *c.* 1938, says: 'The phenomenon is easily explained if these words were originally lacking, and were later supplied from the other accounts, especially from Paul; but if these words had stood originally in Luke, we cannot explain why they could have been omitted later by anyone, while all the other accounts were left uncontested. But that means that the original text of Luke did not contain these words.'

[2] Op. cit., p. 262.

institution of the sacrament of the Lord's Supper, as well as a judgment that it is quite credible that Luke should have published a representation of the last Supper sharply at variance with that of the other accounts.

Although the scepticism which comes to expression at this point is not isolated from a broader scepticism with regard to the testimony of the New Testament writings regarding Christ and the origins of Christianity, I must be content here with pointing out that it is hardly likely that a radical divergence of viewpoint with regard to the institution of the Lord's Supper would have developed in the early church. In particular, considering the association of Luke with the apostle Paul and his opportunities of information regarding the life of the church of his day, it is incredible that he would have been unacquainted with the practice of the church as Paul reports it in I Cor. xi. 23 ff., and would have published a contradictory version of it. For Paul's testimony, it should be observed, concerns not the observance of a segment of the church as that had developed several decades after the death of Christ, but a view which he must have taught and maintained throughout his Christian career and which he insists is clothed with the authority of the Lord Himself. Like the doctrine of the resurrection of Christ, this is hardly a matter on which Paul would have differed substantially from the other apostles (cf. I Cor. xv. 11). Quite apart from the common testimony of the Gospels, therefore, there is good reason to conclude that there must have been in the early church a normative tradition and interpretation. So if Luke's association with the apostle Paul were less intimate than the evidence appears to demand, and even if the Lucan authorship of this Gospel were rejected, it would still not follow that the author of Luke-Acts, who at so many points gives proof of his competence to report Christian tradition accurately, would have been likely to go astray on this feature of Christian worship.[1]

[1] *Didache* 9 mentions the cup before the broken bread, and does not specifically associate the death of Christ with the Eucharist. Thus it is thought to have points of contact with the Lucan representation according to the Western Text as well as to point to the flexibility of observance at the close of the first century. Cf. Creed, op. cit., pp. 262, 265.

The *Didache* account is indeed distinctive. As a matter of fact, the broken bread, as well as the cup, is not referred to the death of Christ, and hence it differs

Most earnest consideration must be given, therefore, to the possibility that the textual variation is the result of a scribal error of omission. The ancient scribes were not distinguished for their archæological knowledge or their exegetical penetration, and hence they often stumbled over superficial difficulties and fashioned 'easier' readings. May that not be the case here? May not the second reference to the cup have been confusing to a second century scribe who knew only of the single cup in the other accounts and of the single cup employed in the current Christian observance of the sacrament? That the double cup would have been disconcerting to some early Christians is shown from the fact that the Syriac Peshitto Version solves the problem by omitting verses 17 and 18, an excision which had the advantage of preserving essentially intact the Pauline form. But one can quite easily imagine that an early scribe, acting with less conscious deliberation, might rather clumsily have removed the reference to the second cup.[1]

That which might have confused a scribe would, however, have been altogether intelligible to one who was acquainted with the Jewish celebration of the passover. There can be no question that Luke is underscoring the fact that the Passover was the occasion of whatever was taught and done that was new and distinctive. Among modern scholars who have been concerned with the problem of the date of the death of Christ, there has developed the view that certain data of Matthew and Mark may best be understood on the supposition that the occasion was prior to the Passover. But no one can doubt that Luke is depicting the occasion as the Passover meal. For example, he reports Jesus as saying, after He had sat down with the apostles, 'With desire I

essentially from Luke at this point. But the testimony of the *Didache*, in spite of its claims, does not possess the historic or normative significance of Lucan tradition. On the credibility of its picture of the apostolic practice, cf. J. Armitage Robinson, *Barnabas, Hermas and the Didache*, 1920, pp. 97 ff., and my *The Apocalypse in the Ancient Church*, 1929, pp. 31 ff.

[1] This would not explain why the concluding words of verse 19 ('which is given for you. Do this in remembrance of me'), words which relate to the bread rather than to the cup, would also have been omitted. See note 3, p. 132. Nevertheless, it seems easier to suppose that a scribe did not make a smooth excision than that Luke, with his fine sense of language and style, would have left verse 19 in the abrupt and awkward state which is admittedly present on the interpolation hypothesis.

have desired to eat this passover with you before I suffer' (xxii. 15).[1] Matthew and Mark concentrate so fully upon the new transactions of the occasion—in stating that it was 'while they were eating' (Mt. xxvi. 26; Mk. xiv. 22) that Jesus instituted the Christian sacrament in His monumental declarations—that the traditional elements of the Jewish passover hardly come to view at all. But may not the greater detail of Luke's account be due to the fact that he is sketching in certain preliminary features of the occasion? As Billerbeck has shown, the first reference to thanksgiving and the giving of *a* cup may provide further evidence that the Lord's Supper was instituted in the course of the passover meal, which, judged by the rabbinic tradition, was by no means restricted to a single cup.[2] Luke, writing in the first century, with abundant opportunity to inform himself concerning the institution of the Supper in Jerusalem, as well as the contemporaneous practices of Judaism, could thus in his account reflect on the historical situation while scribes of a later day might have stumbled at the additional features which were not a part of the Christian observance.

An even more weighty argument concerns the state of the shorter text on the supposition that it was the original. Lk. xxii. 15-18 is beautifully integrated and symmetrical: Jesus speaks of His intense desire to eat the passover before He suffers, but then points to its fulfilment in the kingdom of God; He distributes a cup which He had received, and likewise points to a future action of like character when the kingdom should come. But 19a, which says, 'And He took bread, and when He had given thanks, He brake it, and gave to them, saying, This is my body,' followed by a reference to the presence of the betrayer at the table, leaves the mention of the breaking of the bread, and the reference to His body, hanging in the air. No wonder that several advocates of the interpolation hypothesis conjecture that verse 19a should be deleted, even though there is not a particle of external evidence favouring the omission.[3]

[1] E.g., Creed says that Luke 'gives a definitely Paschal colouring to the Supper itself.' Op. cit., p. 265.

[2] Cf. SBK, IV, p. 75. Pesahim X (*The Babylonian Talmud*, ed. by I. Epstein, 1938, p. 532; cf. pp. 560 ff.) declares that the participant should be given 'not less than four cups'.

[3] E.g. Wellhausen; Blass, op. cit., pp. 179 f. Klostermann allows for this view.

Creed's approach to this situation is most illuminating. He frankly admits that verse 19a 'undoubtedly makes an awkward and abrupt conclusion to the verses preceding' but chiefly because of its presence in all the MSS. and versions does not feel prepared to reject them as an addition.[1] The best argument that Creed can offer, however, in support of his view that Luke retained these words from Mark in spite of the fact that, on his construction, they do not fit easily into his account of the paschal meal, is that it was a part of the tradition from Mark that 'he was unwilling to disturb.' To say the least, it becomes exceedingly difficult on this basis to secure a clear picture of what Luke is supposed to be about. At one moment this Gospel is judged to be radically differing from Mark's version of the Last Supper, but the next so slavishly conservative that it retains a Marcan feature which deeply disturbs the unity of his main approach!

It might be somewhat easier to account for the retention of 19a if Luke were viewed as less exclusively dependent on Mark than is true on Creed's approach, and this condition is in fact fulfilled by advocates of the Four Document Theory. Vincent Taylor, for example, in dealing at length with this question, admits the abruptness of the shorter text and the distinctiveness of perspectives within Luke's account as a whole, as the result of his use of Mark and other sources, and maintains that first Luke added 19a to the original account found in his source (verses 14–18) and, later, copyists added verses 19b, 20, and these are regarded as 'successive attempts to bring the narrative into line with the Marcan and Pauline stories.'[2] But this remains at best a very doubtful hypothesis. If verse 19a represents Luke's own effort to conform his own special viewpoint to that of Mark and Paul, why did he fall so far short of conforming to them as to fail to include the cup which was identified as 'the new covenant in My blood, which is poured out for you'? Why would he have left his own narrative in such an awkward and unintegrated state?

[1] Op. cit., p. 264. He further argues that the position of 19a between verse 16 and verse 17 in the old Latin MSS. b and e does make the words suspect since this peculiar position may be accounted for as due to the desire to assimilate the Lucan account to the other texts (first the bread and then the cup). Moreover, since the words of 19a are in Mark, and Luke used Mark, there is no good ground to regard them as a gloss.

[2] Cf. *Jesus and his Sacrifice*, 1937, p. 176; *Behind the Third Gospel*, pp. 36 ff.

My conclusion, therefore, is that a compelling case for the omission of Lk. xxii. 19b, 20 has not been made. And the difficulties attached to the interpolation hypothesis are so considerable that the rejection of the witness of the type of text usually regarded as superior appears to be quite unjustified. On this view, then, Luke, in common with the other New Testament records which report the institution of the Lord's Supper, reports the teaching of Jesus that through the sacrifice of His body and the shedding of His blood there would be inaugurated a divine covenant transcending the covenant of Sinai, which was also ratified by a sacrifice in which blood was shed.

While the decision regarding the original text of Luke's narrative of the last supper is momentous, it remains doubtful whether, even on the supposition that the shorter text is the original, this Gospel presents an essentially different conception of its meaning. One gets the impression that most supporters of the shorter text have fallen so much under the spell of the impact made by the omission of the reference to the cup, and its redemptive significance, that they have neglected to reflect sufficiently upon the stupendous implications of what Luke is admitted to have set forth in the text which finds universal textual support. In Lk. xxii. 19a, we read that Jesus 'took bread, and when He had given thanks, He broke it, and gave to them, saying, This is My body.' Although, as has been observed, this statement is abrupt, and accordingly presents a serious obstacle to the advocates of the interpolation hypothesis, nevertheless it constitutes a most pregnant utterance concerning the meaning of the death of Christ. For the breaking of the bread, no less unmistakably than the pouring of the cup, points to the violent death which awaited Christ. And Luke is fully as explicit as Matthew and Mark in intimating this fact.

Moreover, Luke, as well as they, declares that Jesus *gave* them the broken bread, and thus discloses that Jesus looked upon His death as that which was undertaken for their sakes. It may not be overlooked that Matthew and Mark make this point without saying that the body of Christ was given on their behalf. Paul is more explicit in reporting that Jesus said, 'This is My body, *which is for you*,' but this does not say anything that is not implicit in the reports of the first two evangelists. And thus also, when the longer text of Luke proceeds to say that the body was 'given for you,' it would be absurd to say that these words, which virtually only echo the declaration that Jesus *gave them* the broken bread, introduce any really new element. All the accounts agree, therefore, in understanding that Christ freely surrendered His body unto death, and that this gift of Himself in death constituted a sacrifice on behalf of His disciples. Regardless, then, of the decision reached with regard to the latter part of verse 19, it may not be affirmed that Luke has dropped the sacrificial language of Mark.[1]

Rudolph Otto, who accepts the shorter text of Luke at this point, must be given credit for recognizing substantially the point just made. Without doubt there are contributing factors bound up with his broader conclusions concerning Christ and the Gospels which affect the decision. These include both his general judgment as to the archaic character of the Lucan testimony and his conclusion that Jesus Himself interpreted His messiahship in terms of the Servant of the Lord concept. But even if these viewpoints are not everywhere acknowledged as salutary, and though one may find good reason for dissenting from other aspects of his construction, he has the merit of construing Lk. xxii. 19a in

[1] H. Lietzmann, *Messe und Herrenmahl*, 1926, p. 216, maintains that Luke pictures the supper merely as a breaking of bread and as being concerned with eschatological hopes. Cf. p. 239. See also Creed, op. cit., pp. 262, 265; Klostermann, p. 208. This conception of the supper is also thought to be reflected in Lk. xxiv. 30, 35, where Jesus is recognized in the breaking of the bread, and in Acts ii. 46, where the Christian fellowship is described as including 'breaking bread in their homes.' Lietzmann says that according to the latter passage, the characteristic cultic practice of the Church was the breaking of bread. Back of the final development of thought and practice concerning the Lord's Supper there stand, accordingly, various influences including the continuation of the table fellowship of Jesus and his disciples, represented particularly by Luke, and the specifically sacrificial conception found in the Pauline teaching.

In view of Lk. xxii. 19a, however, which Lietzmann accepts as original (cf. op. cit., p. 216, note 3 against his HB *I Cor.*[2], p. 60), the significance of the language cannot thus be reduced to the eschatological. Moreover, it is over bold to claim on the basis of Acts ii. 46 that, according to Acts, 'the breaking of bread' exhaustively and particularly describes the cultic practice of the Church. References to breaking of bread may on occasion reflect table fellowship with Jesus, but this would not imply that all do so, and still less that Luke is presenting a special version of the cultic practice. Cf. Lk. ix. 16; Acts xx. 7, 11, xxvii. 35. And in view of the fact that the Lord's Supper was evidently observed in intimate connection with the common meals (cf. I Cor. x and xi), one may not safely conclude that the table fellowship of Acts ii. 46, does not allow for the specific celebration of the sacrament in Pauline terms.

terms of Biblical data. He even states that 'the idea of the ransom for many was precisely the meaning of the distribution of the bread and by the act of distributing the meaning had just been fixed', and his general conclusion is that 'all the essential and constitutive elements of the other accounts are contained in the archaic account,' namely in Luke.[1]

The conclusion that Luke found the redemptive interpretation of the death of Christ uncongenial, or that he was indifferent to it, is also contradicted by Luke's report of Paul's address to the Ephesian elders in which he speaks of the church as 'the church of God which He purchased with His own blood' (Acts xx. 28). Cadbury dismisses the passage in a footnote on the ground that 'it is doubtful both in text and interpretation.'[2] Without minimizing the difficulties of the passage, it is my judgment that neither the textual variations nor the uncertainties of interpretation are such as to obscure the conclusion that the blood of Christ was the redemptive price paid for the church. It is not necessary to argue here in support of my view that 'the church of God' means the church of the divine Christ and that Paul means that Christ acquired the church for Himself at the price of His own blood. For even if 'the church of God' were not intended to designate the church as Christ's, we should still be required to understand that the church became God's possession at the price of the blood of His own Son. The reference to Christ is at least as clear if the reading 'Lord' be accepted.[3]

In the light of these facts and considerations, one may therefore not fairly charge Luke with a special bias against or a basic indifference to the subject of the atonement of Christ because of his failure to quote the ransom saying. He is not indeed writing a dogmatic treatise devoted to an exposition of the doctrine of the atonement as that was taught in the church of his day. The speeches in Acts, for example, while highly doctrinal, are basically summaries of public missionary preaching rather than of the instruction of converts. And in his two-volume work he is aiming to present, in broad strokes, the two main stages of the Lord's activity, and thus considerable stress falls upon the external course

[1] Op. cit., pp. 172, 175; cf. pp. 266 f., 296. Cf. also Dalman, *Jesus-Jeschua*, 1922. pp. 131 f.

[2] *Making*, p. 280, note 2.

[3] See WMMC, p. 166.

of history. But he would obviously have been quite out of sympathy with the modern notion of the Christian message which allocates to Christ and His history, with its climax in His death and resurrection, at best a peripheral place. He plainly believed not only that Christ brought the gospel but also that He was its principal content. For Luke, Christ was pre-eminently the Saviour who came to seek and to save the lost (xix. 9, 10; cf. ii. 11, i, 69, 71, 77; Acts xiii. 23, xvi. 17). He presents the view of radical intolerance with the thought that there is salvation in any other name (Acts iv. 12). And though there is little that explains exactly how men are saved by the cross of Christ and His glorification through the resurrection, the entire disposition of the Gospel, as well as the record of the preaching in Acts, shows that repentance unto remission of sins was preached to the nations only on the basis of the glad tidings of the crucified and risen Saviour (cf. Lk. xxiv. 46; Acts ii. 38, xiii. 38 f.).

THE RESURRECTION NARRATIVE

Although students of the passion narrative of Luke are divided sharply on the question of its dependence upon Mark, the account of the resurrection is so pervasively distinctive that its independence from Mark, except perhaps for the story of the empty tomb, is taken for granted. Indeed, the chief questions relating to Luke's last chapter rise from the fact that it appears to give a picture of the resurrection events utterly different from that of the other synoptics. Whereas Mark and Matthew centre their attention upon an appearance in Galilee, Luke seems to know only of happenings in Jerusalem and its immediate vicinity. The accounts are not as mutually exclusive as they are sometimes thought to be, for in both Mark and Matthew the scene of the stupendous miracle is Jerusalem, and there is in Matthew besides a record of an appearance to certain women after they had left the scene of the empty tomb.[1] Nevertheless, neither Mark nor

[1] Even more basic significance is attached to the belief that the Church originated in Jerusalem by representatives of the 'Jerusalem Hypothesis.' See especially J. Weiss, *Urchristentum*, 1917, pp. 10 ff., 17-71 (*The History of Primitive Christianity*, 1937, I, pp. 14 ff.) and F. C. Burkitt, *Christian Beginnings*, 1924, pp. 76 ff. For evaluation cf. W. P. Armstrong, 'The Place of the Resurrection Appearances of Jesus,' in BTS, 1912, pp. 329-332, and K. Lake in *Christian Beginnings*, II, pp. 170 f.

Matthew contains any intimation of an appearance to the eleven in Jerusalem.

As a corollary of the Galilean Hypothesis, it is commonly maintained that Luke's narrative is clearly secondary. It is thought to have originated some time after the tradition relating to an appearance in Galilee, and to owe its origin to nothing more than the belief that, since Christ was believed to have been raised from the dead, He must have appeared also near the scene of His death. This belief, it is thought, would have found confirmation, if it did not actually originate, from the fact that Jerusalem was regarded as the birthplace of the Christian church. The limits of our present discussion prohibit our undertaking a survey of the history of this hypothesis. It may be recalled, however, that Strauss acutely expressed the problem in the form that, according to one tradition, the disciples are told to go to Galilee in order to see Jesus, whereas, according to the other, they must tarry at Jerusalem.[1] And quite recently, almost exactly one hundred years later, R. H. Lightfoot has written that

> 'all the events narrated in Lk. xxiv between the visit of the women to tomb and the Lord's last parting from the eleven and those that were with them were represented by St. Luke as occurring in or near Jerusalem, and also, we may add, according to the strict letter of the narrative, upon one and the same day, so that as regards both place and time everything set forth in this chapter is brought into very close and intimate connection. . . . The possibility of manifestations of the risen Christ in Galilee is decisively excluded.'[2]

Does Luke in reality exclude the possibility of appearances of the risen Christ in Galilee? If Lk. xxiv is properly construed as Luke's representation of the history of Christ from the time of the resurrection to the ascension, activity in distant Galilee would seem to be beyond the realm of the conceivable. However, such a simple formulation of the disposition of Lk. xxiv fails to take into adequate account several important considerations. These involve the testimony of Paul, the witness of Luke's own narrative in Acts, and the manifest aims and methods of his own Gospel.

[1] *Das Leben Jesu*, 1840, II, pp. 588 f., 606 ff. (Eng. trans., III, pp. 327 f., 343 f.)
[2] *Locality and Doctrine*, pp. 78 f.

In the first place, the apostle Paul, in setting forth the gospel which he had received, indicates that according to the earliest known Christian tradition there were many appearances of the risen Lord. With this tradition in view it is unreasonable to suppose that Luke, or any other of the evangelists, was intending to list all the manifestations of the risen Christ which were generally known. The basic significance of the Pauline testimony to the resurrection of Christ is recognized by critics of the Gospel narratives, and it is often alleged that Paul proves some of the testimony of the Gospels to be in error. But is justice done to the impact of Paul's witness to the primitive tradition concerning the resurrection? If Paul were reporting his own individual faith and experience merely, or were only recording an isolated tradition, the situation would be different. But the fact is that he claims to present Christian tradition which was current as early as the days of his own first contacts immediately after his conversion with the Christian church, the church of the apostles, the church which recognized Jerusalem as its centre.[1] And since Luke was not isolated from Paul or that church, there is in advance a strong improbability in the supposition that his brief account in Lk. xxiv is presented as a summary of the known facts.

Nor, in the second place, has Luke's own account in Acts i been allowed its due weight by those who have insisted that Lk. xxiv excludes more than a single day's appearances at the scene of Christ's death. Although 'the former treatise' included in its scope 'all that Jesus began both to do and to teach until the day in which He was received up,' and the Acts is basically occupied with the activity of the exalted Lord through the Holy Spirit whom He sent forth on the day of Pentecost, the line is not drawn so sharply at the ascension as to exclude reflection within Acts upon the final events of the historical career of Christ upon earth. Thus the references to the resurrection and to the ascension of Christ in Acts i serve to centre attention upon the future programme of the Lord but also supplement in a significant manner the knowledge of the things which Jesus did 'until the day in which He was received up.' The ascension is given the briefest reference at the close of Luke, but is set forth with considerable explicitness in Acts. Similarly, the

[1] Cf. I Cor. xv. 1 ff., 11; Gal. i. 18 f.; ii. 1 ff.

testimony to the resurrection in Acts i, supplements in important particulars the Gospel narrative. In Acts i, in keeping with its generally forward look, prominence is given to the future significance of the apostles, and it was appropriate in this connection to mention their election and commission as a kind of recapitulation of the history of their association with Christ. Of utmost significance for their qualifications was the fact that Christ had 'showed Himself alive after His passion by many proofs, appearing unto them by the space of forty days, and speaking the things concerning the kingdom of God' (Acts i. 3). Since Luke here intimates that there were forty days of contact between Jesus and His disciples between His resurrection and ascension, and he moreover does not restrict the appearances to any particular locality, it would be surpassing strange if Lk. xxiv were intended to be understood as restricting this history to a single day in Jerusalem.

Those who nevertheless interpret Lk. xxiv in such terms are certainly not completely oblivious to the force of the testimony of Acts i. But they are compelled in this exigency to maintain that Luke, perhaps under the influence of a written source or a tradition which came to his attention after he had completed the Gospel, contradicted his earlier record. If Luke and Acts could be shown to be two sharply isolated works, separately conceived and definitely demonstrating independent influences in their execution, such an explanation might possess a degree of plausibility. In the light of the facts, however—that Luke and Acts, as the research of recent decades has emphatically confirmed, not only are demonstrably in remarkable agreement in form and outlook, but also may most satisfactorily be viewed as constituting not two separate treatises but a single work—the view that Luke would introduce at the beginning of Acts a flagrant contradiction of the narrative in the final chapter of the Gospel is most improbable. In continuing his narrative to Theophilus concerning 'those matters which have been fulfilled among us,' Luke makes no apology for mistakes or misrepresentations in his former treatise. Consequently, it would be most unscientific to dismiss the testimony concerning the forty days in one's interpretation of Lk. xxiv, unless the evidence in support of the charge of discrepancy were actually overwhelming.

When one finally turns to examine Lk. xxiv, one encounters another basic defect in the modern approach. This amounts virtually to a failure to take seriously into account at this point what one should observe as to the evident aims and methods of the evangelist in the preceding twenty-three chapters. As attention is directed to the framework of Luke's Gospel in comparison with that of the other synoptics, it appears again and again that the third evangelist is least concerned with the chronological and topographical setting of the incidents and teachings which he reports. He is not, as has been shown above, indifferent to the matter of framework, but he is content frequently to introduce discourse or narrative material without reference to time or place, and hence it is impossible to speak in terms of a definite itinerary or an established sequence of events in most contexts. There is cause for wonder whether recent critics of the Lucan narrative have been fully emancipated from the older view that the evangelists were intending to set forth the precise historical framework of Jesus' life or, on a lower view of their trustworthiness, that they aimed to construct a precise framework of their own. Whatever the factors may be that are responsible for such views of the intent of the evangelists, it is my judgment that the more closely one attends to Luke's method in narrating all that precedes the resurrection story, the less ready one will be to conclude that in chapter xxiv he definitely meant to narrate the events of but a single day.

Although the considerations just reviewed suggest the propriety of caution, the question remains to be considered how Lk. xxiv may be understood as allowing for a longer interval than one day between the resurrection and the ascension. There can be no question that the resurrection itself and the interview on the way to Emmaus are placed on the first day of the week (Lk. xxiv. 1-35; cf. verse 13). The appearance to the disciples recorded in Lk. xxiv. 36-43 is also intimately associated with what precedes, and can hardly be thought of as having occurred later than at evening or during the night at the close of that first day. On the other hand, the charge not to depart from Jerusalem until after the outpouring of the Holy Spirit (Lk. xxiv. 49; cf. Acts i. 4) appears decisively to exclude any later journey to Galilee. Such a journey and the other events of the forty days apparently must fall between Lk. xxiv. 43 and xxiv. 49. Here various possibilities are suggested. Plummer, for example, thinks the entire contents of the section including verses 44-49 are to be regarded as *a summary* of the teaching of Jesus to His disciples during the period following His resurrection. On this view, while Luke is recognized as being aware of the fact that Jesus associated with the disciples over a period of forty days, the evangelist is seen to be content to narrate briefly the first and final appearances to the disciples and to indicate the nature of the message which He taught within this period. Other interpreters allow for the events of the forty days by finding a point of transition at verse 44 or verse 45, or at still other points. The most plausible of these is that verse 44 introduces a new paragraph, and is not meant to be immediately associated with what precedes.[1] Luke himself does not mark out the sequence of events or indicate points of transition, but with an eye upon his characteristic literary method one may infer that he does not rigidly exclude a flexible construction of the course of events.

Although, therefore, the resurrection narrative in Luke is selective and compressed, it remains true that the Gospel places a remarkable emphasis upon the fact of the resurrection. Since the death of Christ is constantly proclaimed in connection with the resurrection, the evaluation of the peculiar stress upon the resurrection will also have implications for our understanding of the subject of the death of Christ which has been so largely before us in this chapter. And indeed this evaluation will bear significantly upon our total thought with regard to Luke's proclamation of the gospel.

The solemn pronouncements concerning the approaching passion and death of the Son of Man, as reported by the other evangelists as well as Luke, point to the resurrection as an act by which the One who was to be set at nought of men would be exalted by God. But this motif comes to much fuller and more explicit expression in Luke's treatment of the resurrection than in the other accounts.

[1] The particle δέ might conceivably link the contents of verse 44 closely with that which precedes, but its use in Luke illustrates the fact that it may introduce a new situation and new disclosures. Cf. Lk. ii. 1, iii. 1, ix. 1, xvi. 1, xvii. 1. See also Plummer, Klostermann and Creed on Lk. xxiv. 44.

This appears strikingly in his narrative concerning the developments at the empty tomb. The women are not left in doubt as to the true interpretation of what had occurred, for divine messengers explain that the One they were seeking was not to be found among the dead, because He had risen (xxiv. 5 f.). Essentially the same message is reported in Matthew and Mark, but Luke alone intimates that the message recalled the repeated solemn utterances concerning the messianic programme.

> 'Remember how He spoke unto you when He was yet in Galilee, saying that the Son of Man must be delivered up into the hands of sinful men, and be crucified, and the third day rise again. And they remembered His words, and returned from the tomb, and told all these things to the eleven, and to all the rest' (Lk. xxiv. 6-8).

Luke, therefore, far more explicitly than the others, calls attention to the fulfilment of the prophecies of Jesus concerning His passion and resurrection, and thus indicates the integration of the ministry of Christ in its various phases. And the recollection of the prophecies just as this point serves to focus attention upon the conviction that the resurrection of Christ was the goal of His ministry as of Luke's narrative. The resurrection story is in no sense an afterthought, an appendix, to the story of the cross, but rather forms the inevitable climax of the course of events with which Luke was concerned. While there was a divine necessity which underlay the march to the cross at Jerusalem, it was unthinkable that the divine Servant should not triumph over death.

The silence of Luke with regard to a reunion with the disciples in Galilee, recorded by both Matthew and Mark, is striking. He is, of course, completely self-consistent on this point, for he also omits any reference to Christ's prophecy concerning the reunion spoken on His way to Gethsemane.[1] In considering this silence, one is faced with the alternative that the evangelist had never heard of an appearance there—an intrinsically difficult hypothesis —or that he decided to omit that tradition and to confine his account to manifestations in and about Jerusalem. The question would still be an open one on the latter alternative whether or not the difference in the scene of the appearance involves on

[1] Mt. xxvi. 32, xxviii. 7, 10, 16; Mk. xiv. 28, xvi. 7.

Luke's part a deliberate rejection of the Galilean tradition and an effort to establish, or confirm, a tradition which confined Jesus' post-resurrection activity to Judæa. It is quite possible that Luke, without doctrinal and historical bias, chose to select, from the many appearances of the risen Christ known to the Christian church, certain manifestations of which he personally could testify on the basis of his contacts with Christians in Judæa.

While, then, Luke might remain silent on the Galilean tradition without prejudice to its historicity, the fact remains that the content of the message to the women as reported by Luke contains unique elements. R. H. Lightfoot speaks of the Lucan form as involving 'a very daring change.'[1] Luke is thought to have freely manipulated the traditional material as found in Mk. xvi. 7 by the substitution of Lk. xxiv. 6 f. When it is argued in support of this view that the mention of 'Galilee' in Lk. xxiv. 6 is due to his knowledge of Mark and a compulsion to be faithful to the older tradition, or, as Creed says, that it 'is no doubt an echo of the Marcan source,' the reasoning is particularly implausible. If Luke is as radically independent of Mark as is assumed at this point, how can he have been so slavishly dependent upon him as is implied here? Moreover, the Lucan words in xxiv. 6 f. to which exception is taken are not Luke's version of the message for the disciples. On the contrary they form a supplement to the words spoken to the women in explanation of the empty tomb. And in view of the integration of this message with the pronouncements concerning the approaching passion and resurrection, they do not form an excrescence upon the tradition or constitute a bold change. If there is a surprising feature in this connection, it is that Matthew and Mark fail to include specific recollection of the fulfilment of the solemn pronouncements of Jesus.

The extensive Lucan story concerning the encounter with the two disciples on the way to Emmaus sounds the same note as the angel's message to the women at the tomb. The disappointed disciples who had supposed that Jesus was the One who should redeem Israel, and who were bewildered by reports that had reached them that He was alive, are told:

'O foolish men, and slow of heart to believe in all that the

[1] See *History and Interpretation*, pp. 166 f.; *Locality and Doctrine*, pp. 80 ff.

> prophets have spoken! Behoved it not the Christ to suffer these things, and to enter into His glory?' (Lk. xxiv. 25 f.).

Reflection upon the sufferings and death of Christ, apart from contemplation of His glory, left men in despair and disillusionment. But so to think of Jesus was not to recognize Him as the Christ. For the Christ, the Anointed of the Lord, there could be no supposition of failure and defeat. Consequently, in the historical situation, the resurrection rather than the crucifixion is in the foreground of attention.

Finally, in Luke's report of the message of Jesus to His disciples, the resurrection is seen to be the goal of His ministry to which the Scriptures and Christ's own teaching pointed:

> 'These are My words which I spoke unto you, while I was yet with you, how that all things must needs be fulfilled, which are written in the law of Moses, and the prophets, and the psalms, concerning Me. Then opened He their minds, that they might understand the scriptures; and He said unto them, Thus it is written, that the Christ should suffer, and rise again from the dead the third day . . .' (Lk. xxiv. 44 ff.).

It does not come as a surprise, therefore, that Luke's record of the apostolic preaching in the Acts is occupied to a large extent with the resurrection of Christ, while the passion of Christ is introduced more succinctly. The apostolic message thus reflects basically the perspective of Jesus' own outlook upon the climax of His career, and in turn the message serves to illumine the origin of the formation of the written Gospels. One must allow for differences of emphasis in the Gospels, as in the reports of the apostolic preaching, taking account of the somewhat different historical occasions of the utterances and the individuality of the spokesmen. Thus the stereotyped character of the proclamation of the gospel of Jesus Christ must not be exaggerated. There is even somewhat of a difference in emphasis between the final chapters of Luke and his reports of the early preaching, which suggests that the first preaching of the Christian missionaries gave great prominence to the evidential significance of the resurrection of Christ for the understanding of Christ and Christianity, while the more finished publication of 'the things fulfilled among us' in the Gospel as appropriately dwelt more fully upon the saving significance of Christ's passion. But it must be reiterated that in all the real goal is the exaltation of Christ through the resurrection, and the full realization of this fact has left its impact upon the disposition of Luke's Gospel.

That Luke somewhat distinctly accents the glory of Christ through His exaltation receives confirmation from a quite different angle. Luke alone of the evangelists brings his Gospel to a close with a real departure of Jesus from His disciples; he alone reports the ascension. The words 'and He was carried up into heaven' are lacking in certain manuscripts, and they are omitted in certain modern editions of the New Testament. But even if they are a gloss, they represent an entirely correct understanding of what Luke meant when he said that 'while He blessed them, He parted from them' (xxiv. 51). That Luke has the ascension in mind is clear, in the first place, from the testimony of Acts, which not only narrates the ascension in some detail as the event which marked His departure (Acts i. 9 ff.), but explicitly views the ascension as the *terminus ad quem* of Luke's Gospel, concerned as it was with 'all that Jesus began both to do and to teach, until the day in which He was received up' (Acts i. 1 f.). But, even without the benefit of this testimony, it would have been quite clear that in xxiv. 51 Luke had in mind far more than a casual departure of Jesus; it was a departure which caused them to return to Jerusalem with great joy, evidently to await the fulfilment of the promise that, tarrying in the city, they would be clothed with power from on high (xxiv. 49). In their exultant joy as they awaited that great event, they 'were continually in the temple, blessing God.' The Father's promise was to be fulfilled, and they recognized in Jesus' parting the event which would hasten the further manifestation of the divine action on their behalf. The Gospel according to Luke, therefore, ends on a triumphant note, a note of fervent joy, and of praise at the contemplation of the marvellous works of God.

To some extent the Acts promotes understanding of this distinguishing feature of the Gospel. Luke was an author whose literary goal comprehended the Acts as well as the Gospel. The exaltation of Christ through the resurrection and ascension did not merely serve him to round off the publication of the Gospel. As his occupation with these events in the first chapter of Acts especially intimates, they are viewed pre-eminently as the great foundational facts which undergird the new order. They are historical events, but with eschatological significance, ushering in a new era marked by the extraordinary manifestation of the Holy Spirit whom the exalted Lord at God's right hand had sent forth. Hence, even Luke's literary goal helps to explain the accent upon Christ's exaltation.

But in his case, without doubt, the literary aims were rooted in his outlook upon the unfolding of history according to the divine plan. As a Christian man Luke shared the faith which joyfully acknowledged Jesus as Lord and Christ, who had entered upon a new and victorious phase of His messianic ministry through His exaltation to the right hand of God (Acts ii. 35 f.). A still more glorious phase of His messianic activity would be ushered in by His return (cf., for example, Acts i. 11, iii. 21); and it had been preceded by his ministry as the Servant, the Holy and Righteous One, the Christ of God (cf., for example, Acts iii. 13, 14, 18). In these distinctions with regard to the ministry of Jesus—past, present and future—there was implicit a broad conception of the unfolding of the divine action in Christ. But the Christ who was invoked, confessed and worshipped by the faithful, was the living Lord. Though He was remembered as the One who on their behalf had surrendered His life unto death, and had ratified the new covenant in His blood, and though there was a sober realization that the perfect consummation was to be manifested only in the future manifestation of the rule of God, their present faith in Him as the Lord bound the elements of remembrance and hope together and afforded a present assurance of grace and righteousness through faith in His name. That living, abiding, dynamic faith of Luke gives perspective to his entire undertaking in proclaiming Jesus as the One 'that died, yea rather was raised from the dead' (cf. Rom. viii. 34).[1]

[1] Cf. my *The Areopagus Address*, pp. 48, 12 f., Tyndale Press, London, 1950.

CHAPTER VIII

THE KINGDOM AND THE MESSIAH

IN this concluding chapter our attention will centre upon the message of Christ according to Luke. As in the other Synoptics that message may be most concisely summed up in terms of the coming of the kingdom of God.[1] But there also emerges, in the context of the evangelical proclamation of the Messiah, Jesus' own claims of messiahship expressed in word and deed. These are not two messages, however, but one; and hence there is no more significant question of interpretation than that of the relation of the coming of the Christ to the manifestation of the kingdom.

To a considerable extent this theme has been evaluated in the preceding chapters. The discussion of the passion narrative and of its climax in the resurrection of Jesus has thrust into the foreground the Christological question, and has demonstrated that, though the gospel might be formulated tentatively in terms of the coming of the kingdom, that kingdom is so indissolubly bound up with the ministry of Christ, and even identified with His person, that the gospel comes to find expression in distinctly personal terms. The decisive work of salvation is Christ's, the action of the Son of Man who 'came to seek and to save the lost' (Lk. xix. 10). This work itself has such transcendent significance that its accomplishment by the Messiah implies that He is thought of in transcendent terms, and since He is none less than the divine Messiah there is a guarantee that the kingdom will come to realization as He fulfils His ministry.

The leading issues involved in the subject of the Messiah and the kingdom have been in view at least as early as the Lucan narrative of the appearance and rejection at Nazareth, which was considered at length in chapter IV. The Christological aspect of the message is distinctly present, for it is evident that the coming of a new order coincides with the presence and activity of Christ. Nevertheless, this aspect is presented with considerable reserve,

[1] Cf. Lk. iv. 43 ('I must preach the good tidings of the kingdom of God to the other cities also: for therefore was I sent'), viii. 1, ix. 11. See also Lk. ix. 2, 60.

and the accent falls at this point upon the dawn of the new age of righteousness and grace rather than upon the coming of the Messiah. Utilizing one of the climactic prophecies of Isaiah, the Lord discloses by His extraordinary comment that the eschatological age, when injustices and other consequences of sin would be overcome and which was proclaimed as realizable and assured of realization only because of the free, sovereign grace of the Holy One of Israel, was in process of fulfilment. Here, too, there is restraint in presenting the theme of the establishment of the divine rule. No account is taken at Nazareth of the final consummation of the kingdom associated with the coming of the Son of Man on the clouds of heaven. And it remains expressed basically in the prophetic language of the Old Testament rather than in the more didactic language of the New Testament which has been fashioned within the crucible of the development of stupendous and momentous historical events. Hence the teaching at Nazareth is not programmatic for the Gospel; it does not summarize the teaching of Jesus. It serves, rather, effectively to introduce it. Reflection upon Isaiah's delineation of the coming kingdom indicates the pattern of the kingdom as proclaimed by Christ and as it begins to come to realization through His deeds. But one must undertake an examination of the actual teaching of our Lord within the entire Gospel to take in its entire sweep and to bring the whole into sharp focus.

Advantage may be taken here of the results arrived at in the study of the teaching as recorded in Mark and Matthew. Particularly on the basis of the data in Matthew, it appears that various aspects of the manifestation of the kingdom must be distinguished. The kingdom is one, and it may be recognized as being basically 'eschatological' in view of its consummation through divine interposition. But no contradiction is involved in recognizing that, prior to the consummation at the end of the age, there have been significant preliminary manifestations of the kingdom which are also the consequence of decisive divine action in history. The divine action in view is in and through Christ, and thus the stages of the coming of the kingdom correspond with the stages of the ministry and activity of Christ. The action of the returning Son of Man ushers in the kingdom in its final glory and power. His exaltation to God's right hand also constitutes a most signal triumph of God in the accomplishment of His purposes of redemption, and hence a specific historical turning point in the work of making actual the divine rule. But even prior to this development the very presence of the Son of Man upon earth, and His victory over the works of Satan, signalizes that the kingdom has actually come.[1]

THE COMING OF THE KINGDOM

Do not the Lucan data require the same three-fold distinctions? In most instances where Luke refers to the kingdom, the question of stages of manifestation is left quite unsettled. When Jesus says, for example, 'Blessed are ye poor, for yours is the kingdom of God,' the kingdom of consummation may be in view but quite as well also its prior realizations in history.[2] There are, however, other utterances which unambiguously have in view a coming that is future from the point of view of Jesus' utterance. The kingdom is announced as having drawn nigh (Lk. x. 9, 11, xxi. 31); the disciples are taught to pray, 'Thy kingdom come (Lk. xi. 2). Such references need not indeed be restricted to the final consummation. But the expectation of the future also includes the hope of the establishment of a new and final order in which the pious dead will participate. Jesus looks forward to a fulfilment of His eating and drinking with the disciples in the kingdom of God (Lk. xxii. 16, 18, 29 f., xiv. 15), and teaches that Abraham, Isaac and Jacob and all the prophets will be seen therein (Lk. xiii. 28 f.; cf. xxiii. 42 f.).

Although, then, the strictly eschatological aspect of the kingdom is plainly in view, there is a remarkable emphasis upon the phase of the kingdom which has been realized in the history of Christ. Since Lk. vii. 24 ff., 28, xvi. 16 and xi. 20 closely parallel Mt. xi. 7 ff., 12, xii. 28 in showing that through the work of Christ the kingdom had come, and men were entering it, this perspective does not find its original expression in Luke.[3] Nevertheless, as the preaching at Nazareth has shown, it is placed in the foreground in this Gospel. Most pointed of all is the distinctive

[1] This subject, especially as it is presented in Matthew, has been treated at some length in WMMC, Chapter VIII.

[2] Lk. vi. 20. Cf. viii. 10, ix. 62, xix. 16 f., 24 f., xiii. 18 f., 20 f.

[3] On the interpretation of the passages in Matthew see WMMC, pp. 244 ff.

saying of Lk. xvii. 21, 'The kingdom of God is in your midst.' Here Jesus points to the radical misunderstanding of the nature of the kingdom displayed by the Pharisees. While they supposed that its manifestation was completely future, and conceived of it as so much a part of the present world-order that one might calculate the time of its coming, Jesus taught that it was of such an utterly different nature that it would come only through a sudden divine act, and indeed was even then in their very midst.[1]

In view of the plain testimony to the kingdom as realized, at least incipiently, through the ministry of Christ upon earth, it is remarkable that there is little or no explicit reflection upon the fashion in which the kingdom of God was to enter upon a new stage of realization through the exaltation of Christ. That this thought is dwelt upon in Matthew may well be explained by its teaching concerning the establishment of the Church.[2] Nevertheless, in other ways the same basic perspective appears. Luke, too, pointedly emphasizes the supreme dignity and power which the Son of Man will occupy at God's right hand (Lk. xxii. 69). He also stresses the fact that through the resurrection the Son of Man would enter into His glory (Lk. xxiv. 26; cf. ix. 22, xviii. 31 ff., xxiv. 46). And he points forward to the new era which would be inaugurated by the Spirit when He was sent forth by the exalted Christ (Lk. xxiv. 49; cf. Acts i. 8, ii. 33). Moreover, it is clear from the place which the church occupied in Acts as the new people of God constituted through the redemption of Christ and the eschatological manifestation of the Spirit (Acts xx. 28, ii. 1 ff.)

[1] Bultmann, *Jesus*, 1926, p. 39; *Die Geschichte der synoptischen Tradition*, 2te Aufl., 1931, pp. 24, 128, interprets ἐστίν as a prophetic present in the interest of conforming the passage to the 'consistent' eschatological view of the kingdom. K. L. Schmidt in TWNT, I, p. 587 says it has nothing to do with the question of time, but only with the rejection of omens. On the other side, cf. R. Otto, op. cit., pp. 131 ff. If there were no other evidence in the teaching of Jesus that the kingdom was regarded as already significantly present, and if in the present context there were intimations that a future coming were as a matter of fact clearly in view, this interpretation of the present tense might be allowable. However, the use of the present rather than the future creates a definite presumption in favour of understanding it as an actual present. And that a future meaning cannot have been in Jesus' mind is shown most simply from the consideration that the words 'The kingdom of God will be in your midst' would be pointless as a reply to the question of the Pharisees concerning the time of the coming of the kingdom.

[2] Cf. WMMC, pp. 234 ff.

that, in the last analysis, Luke also looked upon the church as a climactic carrying forward of the kingdom that appeared in the very midst of the Jewish people through the presence and activity of Christ. In view of these considerations, it is not at all incongruous to judge that the church may be included within the kingdom in the words, 'But I tell you of a truth, There are some of them that stand here who shall in no wise taste of death until they see the kingdom of God' (Lk. ix. 27).[1]

On the background of this survey of the structure of the historical realization of the kingdom of God according to Luke, one may evaluate the charge that Luke tones down the earlier Christian emphasis upon the imminence of the kingdom.[2] Appeal is made particularly to Lk. ix. 27, xxii. 69, xix. 11, and xxi. 8 to substantiate this judgment, but obviously there is presupposed a certain judgment as to the eschatological perspective of Mark and other early witnesses. And it is my conviction that, apparently because of the vogue obtained by the 'consistent' eschatological viewpoint, extremely one-sided opinions have developed. On the basis of the dogma that Christ and the early Christian Church acted on the assumption that the end of the world was necessarily to come momentarily, thoroughgoing reconstructions of the origins of Christianity have been undertaken. There have been confident assertions that at first there could have been no interest in external organization, in a written expression of the faith, and in the formation of the New Testament Canon. Such theories have been spun out of most inadequate interpretations of the pertinent data. Broadly speaking, indeed, the outlook was eschatological. One encounters frequent admonitions to be found watchful and waiting. But the warning to live in expectation of the return of the Son of Man because He would come as a thief in the night (1 Thes. v. 2) does not imply that He would necessarily return so soon that provision for earthly needs and eventual wants would be of no concern. In fact the very insistence upon the uncertainty of the time of His return would stand as a constant warning not to determine in advance precisely when the hour would strike. The position of 2 Thessalonians may not therefore be held to disclose a modified eschatological perspective. It

[1] On these passages and their synoptic parallels cf. WMMC, pp. 238 ff.
[2] E.g. Creed, op. cit., pp. lxxii f. Cf. also Cadbury, *Making*, pp. 291, 293 f.

protests against certain foolhardy and disastrous deductions from what had been taught, and intimates that there would be events of catastrophic proportions in the midst of the present world before the return of Christ (2 Thes. ii. 1 ff.). But this implies only that some Christians had drawn wrong inferences from Paul's teaching, not that Paul had altered his own position.

Nor does the teaching in Mark support the one-sided conception of the imminence of the kingdom. For Mark also contains the teaching that the 'end' will by no means come before the fulfilment of certain highly significant prophecies, including that concerning the proclamation of the gospel to all the nations (Mk. xiii. 7, 10). And in general Mark places such an emphasis upon the transforming meaning of the ministry of the Son of Man upon earth and upon the resurrection as the goal of His ministry that his testimony gives far greater prominence to eschatology that is realized before the end than to that which awaits realization through the parousia.[1]

Creed cites Lk. ix. 27 and xxii. 69 in declaring that 'the more striking Marcan prophecies of the *imminence* of the kingdom are softened.'[2] It is not self-evident, however, that Mark's 'until they see the kingdom of God come with power' (ix. 1) stresses imminence more than Luke's 'until they see the kingdom of God' (Lk. ix. 27). Coming 'with power' may quite well be distinguished from coming 'with great power and glory' (Mk. xiii. 26). And in view of the use of the word 'power' for the miracles of Christ for example in Mk. vi. 2, 5, 14), and its application to the resurrection in Mk. xii. 24, it would be quite appropriate to characterize the preliminary manifestations of the kingdom as a coming 'in power.' The appeal to Lk. xxii. 69 is somewhat more impressive since Luke, as distinguished from Matthew and Mark (Mt. xxvi. 64; Mk. xiv. 62), omits at this point any reference to the coming of the Son of Man on the clouds of heaven. Since, however, he includes frequent references to the coming of the Son of Man in glory (Lk. ix. 26, xvii. 24, 26, 30, xviii. 8, xxi. 27, 36), great care must be exercised not to overstress the significance of the omission at this point. Mark does not say or imply that the coming with the clouds of heaven would follow immediately upon the 'sitting at

[1] On the eschatological perspective of Mark cf. WMMC, pp. 109 ff.
[2] P. lxxii.

the right hand of Power,'[1] and so Luke's omission may be merely in the interest of simplicity and clarity of expression. It was sufficient for his purpose to report merely the statement concerning Christ's exaltation to God's right hand as indicative of His vindication and victory.

Creed contends that Lk. xix. 11 and xxi. 8 'betray an attitude of some suspicion towards those who look for an immediate fulfilment of the hope.'[2] In the former passage, where Luke says that Jesus proceeded to tell the parable of the pounds 'because He was nigh to Jerusalem, and because they supposed that the kingdom of God was immediately to appear,' there is indeed an implied disagreement with an eschatological outlook which is in danger of losing sight of tasks to be accomplished on earth while men were waiting for the coming of the kingdom. But this is hardly distinctive of Luke. And though Lk. xxi. 8 disapproves of false Christs who say, 'The time is at hand,' the polemic is more basically directed against the false Christs than against the words as such. Though the words employed are not given in Mark, that Gospel quite as definitely as Luke warns in this discourse against those who would lead the disciples astray with premature and erroneous reports concerning the appearance of Christ (cf. Mk. xiii. 5 ff.).

There does not therefore appear to be a solid case for the contention that Luke has softened the prophecies of the imminence of the kingdom in the interest of adjusting the eschatological perspective of primitive Christianity to historical developments. The conception of the kingdom of God is by no means restricted to the final consummation, but is in view also when earlier aspects of the realization of the rule of God through the decisive action of Christ are being reflected upon. And in all the records there is a powerful accumulation of testimony to the effect that God's purposes of grace, whereby His rule would be established, His name would be hallowed and His will would be done, did not have to remain merely prospective until the day of the return of the Son of Man on the clouds of heaven, but were decisively, though somewhat preliminarily, realized through the ministry of the Son of Man upon earth and through His entrance upon His glory by the resurrection on the third day.

[1] Cf. H. B. Swete, *Mark*, ad loc. ,and WMMC, pp. 240 ff.

[2] P. lxxii.

THE NATURE OF THE KINGDOM

Of even deeper significance than the question of the time and times of the manifestation of the kingdom is that of its basic meaning: what it reveals concerning God and His relations to men. In a word the kingdom of God may be said to be God-centred and God-given, and thus there are in view the same characteristics which have been observed in connection with our evaluation of the prophetic Scripture read by our Lord in the synagogue at Nazareth.[1] As God-centred, it is basically viewed as the realization of the rule of God, involving the glorification of His holy name and the performance of His righteous will on the part of men; only then can it be a kingdom or realm in which men participate in divine blessings. In congruity with its God-centred character it is God-given; it depends for its realization upon the sovereign grace of God. If God's rule is to be established, He must mercifully bring it to pass. Because it is a reign of righteousness it can never be brought about through the initiative and as a co-operative action of men.[2]

Luke contains a few distinctive sayings that pointedly bear out these characterizations of the kingdom. He reports the saying of Jesus: 'Fear not, little flock; for it is your Father's good pleasure to give you the kingdom' (Lk. xii. 32). Here the non-political, non-worldly character of the kingdom is strikingly disclosed: it belongs to the true disciples of Christ, a little flock, who receive it only because of a disposition of sovereign grace. That the kingdom is constituted by the disposition of God also appears from the saying recorded in Lk. xxii. 29 f. There, according to the rendering of the RV, Jesus declares, 'I appoint unto you a kingdom, even as my Father appointed unto me.' If, as is more probable, as the RV margin and the RSV reflect, the word 'kingdom' is to be construed with the second use of the verb 'appoint,' the passage may be rendered: 'I appoint unto you, as my Father hath appointed unto me a kingdom, that ye may eat and drink at my table in my kingdom.' But the substance remains

[1] See above, pp. 76 ff.

[2] On the basic questions concerning the nature of the kingdom of God see especially G. Vos, *The Teaching of Jesus concerning the Kingdom of God and the Church*, 1903, pp. 90 ff.

the same, for on the second rendering the disciples are assured the blessings of participation in the kingdom because of the fact of Christ's appointment. The choice of the verb translated 'appoint' accents the freedom of the appointment. It may have in view the idea of a testamentary bequest, and then the unilateral character of the action would be stressed. More probably, however, it reflects covenantal bestowal of blessing since the Father would hardly have been spoken of as 'bequeathing' a kingdom to the Son. And then it has all the rich significance bound up with the biblical conception of the covenant established by God with His people, a conception which wonderfully serves to describe the fellowship between God and man, and yet never loses sight of the fact that its establishment is a marvel of divine grace.[1]

Although Luke sets forth the message of the kingdom in absolute terms as God's rule and as God's gift, it is significant that he by no means avoids the use of traditional Jewish language in reporting its expectation. The messianic hope of the disciples on the way to Emmaus, a hope seemingly shattered by the crucifixion, was expressed in the form that Jesus was the one who 'was about to redeem Israel' (Lk. xxiv. 21). And after the restoration of the disciples' confidence in Jesus, the question is still raised whether He would now 'restore the kingdom to Israel' (Acts i. 6). And in speaking of the blessings of His kingdom, Jesus includes the promise that the disciples would 'sit on thrones judging the twelve tribes of Israel' (Lk. xxii. 30; cf. Mt. xix. 28). The formulation of the messianic hope in these terms is misconstrued, however, if it is taken as pointing to a particularistic, essentially Jewish, kingdom in distinction from or alongside of the eternal kingdom. He is not speaking in these connections of a particular phase of the kingdom, but of the kingdom as a whole.

The birth narratives eloquently establish the fact that such language is meant to designate the eternal kingdom inaugurated by the appearance of the Messiah. There it appears that the distinctive terminology is chosen because, quite in keeping with the tenor of the narratives as a whole, the hope is expressed from the point of view of the promises of the Old Testament. Thus the message of the angel to Mary which tells of the significance of His

[1] Cf. also Lk. xvii. 21, which intimates the non-secular character of the kingdom and Lk. i. 33, which characterizes the rule as eternal.

birth relates, in terms of 2 Sa. vii. 12 ff. and Dn. vii. 13 f., the promise that God would give Him the throne of His father David, and emphatically asserts that His reign will be eternal (Lk. i. 32 f.). The pious Simeon was waiting for 'the consolation of Israel' when the Holy Spirit revealed that he would live to see the Anointed of the Lord. And Luke goes on to tell in the words of the *Nunc Dimittis* how Simeon, having seen the babe and received Him into His arms, exults in the fact that His eyes have seen the salvation of God, a salvation which, as Isaiah had prophesied, would be for the Gentiles as well as for the Jews (Lk. ii. 25 ff.). And Anna, the prophetess, having seen Christ in the temple, 'spake of Him to all them that were looking for the redemption of Jerusalem' (Lk. ii. 38). And even at the close of Acts Paul's faith in Christ which had brought him into prison is formulated as 'the hope of Israel' (Acts xxviii. 20). Accordingly, the expectation could be expressed concretely in Old Testament terms as the hope of Israel, the restoration of the kingdom to Israel, the redemption of Israel, the consolation of Israel, and the like, and yet clearly not signify a particularistic manifestation of the kingdom.

Closely associated with the question whether the kingdom is particularistic is that raised by the use of earthly terms in describing the prerogatives of its participants. Notice has been taken of the description of its fellowship and privileges in realistic terms, of eating and drinking at a table and of sitting on thrones (Lk. xxii. 29 f.; cf. xiv. 15 ff.). How are such data to be construed, and what bearing do they have upon the understanding of the nature of the kingdom? On the one hand, it must not be forgotten that biblical eschatology presupposes the doctrine of the creation of the world by God in envisaging a transformed world. It is not a gnostic, spiritualizing doctrine which would find abhorrent the idea of a new heaven and a new earth. The world to come is the world of the resurrection of the dead, in which men, constituted of soul and body, will dwell. On the other hand, that world is a transformed world, suited to the existence of transformed men. Hence care must be taken not to construe the realistic language employed in describing the blessings of the kingdom in a severely physical sense. Account must be taken of the fashion in which within the Bible the glories and blessings of the age to come are characteristically depicted in terms of the restoration of original glories and the repetition of covenant blessings, though it is understood all the while that the world to come, in which the curse has been removed and Christ is seen face to face, is a new world so transcending the glories that have been revealed that it cannot be adequately described in human language. Appropriately then, the language describing the table fellowship of Christ and His disciples is employed to intimate the fellowship of the future age. Similarly the privilege of reigning with Christ is intimated in language drawn from the history of the kingdom upon earth. As the messianic prerogative takes the form that Christ should occupy the throne of His father David, the privilege of those who enjoy the most intimate fellowship with Him in His reign is appropriately expressed in the form that they should sit on thrones judging the twelve tribes of Israel. There is no implication that their thrones were to be physical thrones in a reconstituted theocracy any more than that His throne is conceived in such terms.

While then Luke clearly envisages the kingdom of God as a transcendent new reality, and gives prominence to the universalism of its historical manifestation, it is remarkable how fully Luke retains the Christian sense of continuity with the old order. Only after the most drastic surgery, as Marcion saw, can Luke be appealed to in support of a view of Christianity as a creation out of nothing, as a new beginning in history completely isolated from the Jewish religion. Luke's comprehensive historical work does indeed demonstrate in impressive fashion that Christianity was irreconcilable with the particularism and legalism of contemporaneous Judaism. Nevertheless, as clearly as the other records, he manifests the historical perspective which recognizes that the particularism of the old covenant no less than the universalism of the new was of divine appointment, and that the historical realization of the kingdom through the appearance of Christ by no means relaxed the authority of the law and the prophets. Although Luke perhaps does not fully share Matthew's concern with the theme of the place of Christ in the history of divine revelation, it is clear that his appraisal of the stupendous meaning of the coming of Christ, no less emphatically than Matthew's, presupposed and involved the affirmation of the divine character of the Scriptures of the Jews. The Jesus of Luke, in affirming that 'the law and the prophets were until John' (Lk. xvi. 16), insists also that 'it is easier for heaven and earth to pass away, than for one tittle of the law to fall' (Lk. xvi. 17), and that 'all things must needs be fulfilled, which are written in the law of Moses, and the prophets, and the psalms, concerning Me' (Lk. xxiv. 44). In view of this sense of solid continuity between the action of God under the old covenant and under the new, the formulation of the messianic hope and its realization in Christ and His kingdom in terms of 'the hope of Israel' and of Israel's consolation and redemption does not appear anomalous.

Another question that arises as one gives consideration to the question of the meaning of the kingdom of God for Luke is that of its significance for the world. Since the kingdom of God, as set forth in Luke's record of Jesus' message, is emphatically an historical reality signified as present through the appearance of Christ himself, this matter is of intensely practical concern. Luke has been regarded as presenting essentially a message for the poor and afflicted of this world, and thus a message with strong social implications. Jülicher, for example, maintaining that there is nothing distinctively Pauline in Luke's work, and that the features which show closest agreement with Paul—the universality of salvation and the limitless grace of God—ultimately go back to Jesus himself, finds his own estimate in close agreement with Wellhausen's. This was to the effect that, because of an outspoken sympathy for delinquents and outcasts, Luke commends the Saviour to the sympathy and trust of Greek readers, including particularly the lowest classes.[1] Jülicher further characterizes Luke's religious attitude as one of world-flight, which led to the utilization of a source bearing an Ebionite-Jewish character, and views the future glory as the recompense which will be the portion of those who have hungered and suffered here below.[2] Burkitt similarly speaks of 'a tinge of asceticism' and of 'communism' (by which he seems to mean 'voluntary poverty') as characteristic of Luke.[3]

It is true indeed that Jesus proclaims at Nazareth the message

[1] J. Wellhausen, *Einleitung in die drei ersten Evangelein*, 1905, pp. 69 f.

[2] *Einleitung in das N.T.*[7], 1931, pp. 315 ff.

[3] *The Gospel History and its Transmission*, pp. 210 ff.

that the kingdom of God brings glad tidings to the poor and afflicted (Lk. iv. 18). Moreover, the Gospel gives great prominence to Jesus' friendship with publicans and sinners[1] and His pronouncements of woe upon the rich.[2] But these data provide exceedingly precarious support for the conclusion that the gospel of Jesus was, according to Luke, characterized by an Ebionite social slant or a tendency towards asceticism and communism. There is no glorification of poverty as such and no assurances to the poor that, because they are poor, they will necessarily find happiness. If a state of poverty were being idealized there could hardly be place for the commendation of the rich Zacchaeus for his almsgiving and of almsgiving in general (Lk. xix. 2, 8, xi. 41, xii. 33).[3] The issue is seen to be basically religious rather than basically social. Jesus is not so much concerned to assure the publicans and sinners of the love of God as to rebuke the self-righteous pride of the Pharisees and the complacency of the rich.[4] The advantage which the poor and the publican enjoyed over the rich and the Pharisee was not a positive one, which assured him of the divine favour in this world or in the world to come. It was rather the negative advantage that he was likely to be more ready to receive the kingdom of God because he lacked the self-righteousness and complacency of those who trusted in their religious pre-eminence or material wealth.

In stressing the essentially religious character of this message, however, one must avoid the impression that the kingdom of God as proclaimed by Jesus was without profound social implications. The kingdom is a gift of the Father's good-pleasure, but as it comes in the midst of the world it comes as a rule of righteousness, demanding absolute righteousness of its subjects, and this includes the application, in a thoroughgoing fashion, of the principle of stewardship in all of one's social relationships. It is necessary to stress, however, that this feature is somewhat inferential and secondary. The primary feature of the gospel, without which

[1] Lk. vii. 34; cf. vii. 37, 39, xv. 1, xviii. 10–13, xix. 7.

[2] Lk. vi. 24; cf. xiv. 12, xvi. 1, 19 ff.

[3] The development in the Church at Jerusalem reflected in Acts ii. 44 f., iv. 32 ff., v. 1 ff., vi. 1, was not communism or voluntary poverty. It is described in terms of a voluntary sale and distribution of proceeds to meet the needs which arose. Cf. Acts ii. 34, iv. 34 f., v. 4.

[4] On this point cf. Cadbury, *Making*, pp. 258 f.

the other is meaningless, concerns the tidings of the crucified and risen Saviour in whose name repentance and remission of sins were to be proclaimed (cf. Lk. xxiv. 46, 47). The realization of the kingdom was therefore inconceivable without the accomplishment of the Messiah's task, and the fulfilment of the messianic mission gave assurance of the coming of the kingdom.

THE PERSON OF THE MESSIAH

This brings us to a consideration of the person of Christ in Luke's Gospel. One has no difficulty in recognizing that Luke is presenting the very same Jesus who has been portrayed in the other Synoptics. In all three He is pre-eminently *the divine Messiah.*

A rather extraordinary feature of the modern radical criticism of the Gospels, which may serve well to introduce the discussion of this subject, is that Wrede appealed to a statement recorded by Luke as presenting a Christology more primitive than that contained in Mark itself. The passage is Acts ii. 36 where Peter says: 'Let all the house of Israel therefore know assuredly that God hath made Him both Lord and Christ, this Jesus whom ye crucified.' However, for Wrede's view that according to the earliest form of the Christian messianic faith Jesus became the Messiah only through the resurrection, as also for the view of Schweitzer that Jesus Himself contemplated only a future messiahship, the testimony of Luke as a whole offers no support. The resurrection is marked indeed as the point of Jesus' entrance upon a glorious and triumphant exercise of His lordship, as Christ sat at God's right hand, but there is also a clear recognition of a manifestation of His divine messiahship within the days of His flesh.[1]

Though Luke writes from the point of view of the Christian belief that Jesus entered into His messianic glory through His exaltation, he clearly shared also the conviction of the other evangelists that Jesus had claimed to be and was recognized as being the Messiah from the beginning of His ministry. As in the

[1] Cf. Vos, *The Self-Disclosure of Jesus*, pp. 87, 120. On the self-concealment of Jesus' messiahship, cf. WMMC, pp. 50 ff.; WThJ, Nov. 1947 .X), pp. 83 ff.; Vos, op. cit., pp. 67 ff.; H. N. Ridderbos, *Zelfopenbaring en Zelfverberging*, Kampen, 1946. Ridderbos, pp. 62 f., observes that though the element of concealment is less prominent in Luke than in Mark no different tendency can be detected.

other Gospels, Jesus acknowledged the confession of Peter that He was the Lord's Anointed as being a fitting response to the disclosure of His person and work through His previous activity (Lk. ix. 20). This acknowledgment was also made the occasion for Christ's pronouncements as to the programme of suffering and of the glory that would follow. But Luke alone adds the report that after the resurrection the risen Jesus pointed to the testimony of the Scriptures that the Christ should suffer and enter into His glory (Lk. xxiv. 26, 46; cf. Acts iv. 26, xvii. 3, xxvi. 23). That Jesus was condemned by the Jewish leaders, was crucified, and received the taunts of men because of His claims to be the Messiah (and not merely the prospective Messiah) is abundantly clear (cf. Lk. xxii. 67, xxiii. 2 f., 38, xxiii. 35, 37, 39). Luke, moreover, alone records the acclaim of the crowds at His entry into the city in the precise form, 'Blessed is the King that cometh in the name of the Lord' (Lk. xix. 38). Perhaps the most explicit evidence, however, that Luke views Jesus as the Messiah from the beginning is to be found in the birth narratives. For there the angelic glad tidings tell of the birth in the city of David of 'a Saviour, who is Christ the Lord' (Lk. ii. 11) and Simeon receives the revelation that he should not see death before he had seen the Lord's Christ (Lk. ii. 26).

That Luke believed in Jesus Christ as a supernatural Person will not be disputed, although there exists some difference of opinion as to the exact nature of Jesus' transcendence above mankind. The names and titles which express that superior dignity of Jesus are admittedly somewhat flexible in their meanings. It is therefore necessary to judge their precise connotations in the light of the contexts in which they are found.

So far as the name 'the Son of God' is concerned, the usage coincides so largely with that in Matthew and Mark that it may suffice to treat the evidence merely by way of summary.[1] Satan's use of the name in addressing Jesus (Lk. iv. 3 ff.) and perhaps also that of the demoniacs (Lk. iv. 41, viii. 28) appear to fall short of the level of ontological Sonship. On the other hand, the divine acclamation at the baptism and transfiguration involves a relationship to God that evidently obtains prior to and independently of the Son's mission in the world (Lk. iii. 22 f., ix. 35; cf. xx. 13).

[1] Cf. WMMC, pp. 16 ff.; 211 ff.

For Luke, too, it appears that the Jewish rulers, though representing to Pilate Jesus' claim of messiahship as a threat to the sovereignty of Rome, actually reacted as they did to Jesus' claim, not because of the claim of messiahship as such, but because they understood it as involving a presumption of superhuman dignity (Lk. xxii. 67, 70). Most clearly of all perhaps, the claim to divine Sonship in a form excluding subordination altogether is found in Lk. x. 22, which closely parallels Mt. xi. 27. The Son's knowledge of the Father and the Father's knowledge of the Son are set forth with such exact correspondence and reciprocity, and are moreover made the foundations of their respective sovereign revelational activity, that all subordination is excluded, and the passage constitutes an unambiguous claim of deity on the part of the Son.

To these passages, none of which is completely distinctive of Luke, must now be joined the testimony of Lk. i. 32 and 35. In virtue of the overshadowing of the Holy Spirit which effected the conception of Jesus, He is designated as 'Son of God.' The supernatural conception of Jesus does not by itself, as an isolated fact, establish the deity of Christ. He was divine from all eternity; He could not become more so because of the virgin birth. And it would be appropriate to regard the titles 'Son of God' and 'Son of the Highest' in this context as appropriately given in view of His supernatural conception rather than as precise intimations of deity. On the other hand, it is evident that Luke is witnessing to one who did not have to await any transformation of character to become Son of the Highest (cf. Lk. vi. 35), or even His appointment to, or entrance upon, His office to be designated in this manner, but who from the very outset of His entrance into the world sustained a unique relationship to God. By no means all of the instances of the use of the name 'Son of God' in Luke, accordingly, may be construed as unequivocally signifying equality of the Son with the Father in power and glory. This supreme evaluation is definitely present in the record, however. And without it all the rest would remain inexplicable inasmuch as it is only on the background of a full acknowledgment of His deity that His supernatural entrance into the world and His appointment to perform transcendent religious functions become intelligible. All of these designations of Jesus as Son of God agree in witnessing to Luke's pervasively supernatural view of Jesus' person and activity, and therefore also present an insuperable obstacle in the path of the construction that Luke is a witness to an exclusively future exercise of Christ's messiahship.

It remains true that for Luke Jesus was also the Son of David. There is even an insistence upon the fulfilment of the messianic hope in terms of the Old Testament, which is bound up with previous observations as to the expectation of the coming of the kingdom in Old Testament terms. Although Luke, in distinction from Matthew, is patently not concerned especially to commend Christ to the Jew, his recognition of Jesus as the Son of David provides still another emphatic testimony of the indispensable place which the Old Testament and its formulation of the messianic hope occupied within the faith and life of early Christianity. The question of Jesus in Lk. xx. 41, 'How say they that the Christ is David's Son?' has been understood as a polemic against the interpretation of messiahship in these terms, but without justification. Jesus appeals to Ps. cx in order to sustain His transcendent view of messiahship as involving His lordship over David, but this does not imply that He was not also the Son of David. The firm place which the title occupies in the Christian tradition, including Luke, is proof that the acknowledgements of Him as both Lord and Son of David were considered entirely consistent with each other.[1]

Of special significance in this connection is Luke's description of the messianic hope in Lk. i. 32, 33: 'The Lord God shall give unto Him the throne of His father David: and He shall reign over the house of Jacob for ever; and of His kingdom there shall be no end.' Jesus is introduced as One whose mission could be significantly characterized in terms of the Son of David expectation. The context does not perhaps quite determine when the Son of David was thought of as beginning His reign. Since the context is concerned with the blessed significance of the birth of Christ it would seem more congruous to connect the beginning of His rule with His earthly life than with a future activity connected with the consummation of history. Moreover, in view of the acknowledgement of Jesus as Son of David recorded in Luke (Lk. xviii. 38 f.),

[1] Cf. WMMC, p. 223. For the tradition in Luke see Lk. i. 27, 69, iii. 31, ii. 4, 11; Acts ii. 29 f., xiii. 23; cf. Acts xiii. 34, xv. 16.

and the testimony to Him as the anointed King (Lk. xix. 38), it is hardly plausible to view Lk. i. 32 f. as referring to a distantly prospective kingship. Regardless, however, of one's interpretation of this passage so far as the inception of His reign is concerned, there can be no question that the kingship attributed to Him transcends every political and other merely temporal category. The kingship is *eternal*, and therefore it possesses a transcendent character that corresponds with the view of messiahship which Jesus, by implication, claimed when He taught that the Christ is not merely Son of David but also his Lord.

A transition is thus provided for the consideration of the lordship of Jesus as that appears in Luke. Broadly speaking, there is close agreement with the usage in the other Synoptics.[1] It is employed with considerable reserve in the description of the public ministry. As a title or as a predicate it appears only in the sayings concerning lordship over the sabbath, the Lord's need of the colt, and in the teaching concerning the Messiah's lordship over David.[2] But it is also highly meaningful for the understanding of Jesus' own claims that He was frequently addressed as 'Lord' by disciples who were committed to Him, by those seeking supernatural aid as well as in certain eschatological parables.[3] These data demonstrate that, though Luke records the word of Peter that Jesus had been constituted both Lord and Christ by the resurrection (Acts ii. 36), he likewise regarded Jesus as exercising exalted sovereignty through His messianic activity on earth before the exaltation.

The reserve with which Luke, in common with the other Gospels, designates Jesus as Lord within the public ministry is the more remarkable when the testimony of the birth narratives is recalled. As has been observed in chapter III, even before the birth of Christ Mary is hailed by Elizabeth as 'the mother of my Lord' (Lk. i. 43). And the angelic announcement of the birth to the shepherds takes the form that a Saviour has been born who is 'Christ the Lord' (Lk. ii. 11). Since Luke frequently employs the

[1] See WMMC, pp. 253 ff.

[2] Lk. vi. 5, xix. 31, 34, xx. 42 ff. The instances in the eschatological parables are also significant. Cf. Lk. xii. 41 ff., xiii. 25–28.

[3] It is noteworthy that Luke sometimes uses the word ἐπιστάτα (v. 5, viii. 24, 45, ix. 33, 49, xvii. 13), and that the Semitic forms 'rabbi' and 'rabbouni' do not occur.

name Lord as the designation of God, as for example in recording the prophecy of Simeon that he would live to see 'the Anointed of the Lord' (Lk. ii. 26), it is impossible to avoid the impression that the evangelist is conscious of setting forth the profound mystery that He who was born as the promised Anointed of the Lord was Himself the Lord, and therefore possessed divine sovereignty quite apart from and prior to the establishment of His messianic kingdom.

Another distinctive feature of Luke, which also bears upon one's understanding of his perspective, is that he, as narrator, speaks of Jesus as Lord very frequently, no fewer than fourteen times in fact.[1] That this is characteristically Lucan appears from the observation that Matthew and Mark never refer to Jesus in this way and John does so only two or three times, besides the instances in the resurrection narrative.[2] In view of Luke's reserve elsewhere in his Gospel narrative, he evidently does not aim to create the impression that Jesus frequently spoke of Himself as Lord or was frequently thus addressed during His ministry before the resurrection. He apparently uses the name proleptically to conform to the usage which prevailed in the church when he wrote and to which he may have been somewhat partial. Nevertheless, one cannot fairly exclude the possibility that such a use was fostered by the belief that even before His exaltation to God's right hand, in the days of His ministry upon earth, Jesus was a supernatural person who acted with divine authority and at least occasionally applied the designation to Himself.

The Lucan delineation of Christ also includes the witness that he was the Son of Man. In this Gospel, as in the others, it is consistently used as a self-designation. In Acts, on the other hand, there is a single instance of its use, where Stephen is reported as seeing a heavenly vision of 'the Son of Man standing at the right

[1] Lk. vii. 13, 31, x. 1, 40, xi. 39, xii. 41, 42, xiii. 15, xvii. 5, 6, xviii. 6, xix. 8, xxii. 61 (bis); cf. xxiv. 3. In several of these instances there is some manuscript support, chiefly in the versions, for the omission of this title. It seems more likely, however, that the name was omitted by scribes in the interest of conformity to the customary usage than that it was introduced from liturgical motives. Cf. Creed on vii. 13.

[2] Jn. iv. 1 (where several witnesses including Aleph read 'Jesus'); vi. 23, xi. 2; cf. Jn. xx. 2, 20, xxi. 7, 12.

hand of God' (Acts vii. 56). Although this constitutes a formal exception to the rule that the title is found exclusively on Jesus' lips, the appropriateness of its use is evident when one considers the fact that Stephen's vision corresponds to Daniel's: like Daniel he is beholding the heavenly glory of this exalted figure as He shares the sovereignty of God, and is not speaking of an earthly advent of the Son of Man.[1]

In Luke, as in the other synoptic Gospels, the name appears in every stage of the career of Christ, and further confirmation is provided of the conclusion that there is intimate relationship between the various phases of the coming of the kingdom and the stages of the ministry of Christ. The distinctly eschatological coming of the Son of Man is clearly represented, in part in utterances represented in the Matthean and Marcan narratives, in part in references not closely paralleled in the other accounts.[2] These passages, however, represent only about one-third of the total number in which the title appears. In Lk. xxii. 69 the exaltation of the Son of Man to a place of glory and power at God's right hand is in view, and Luke is silent at this point concerning the return on the clouds of heaven. But in all the rest the predications made concerning the Son of Man relate to His appearance and mission on earth. Most of these, including especially the pronouncements concerning the suffering and humiliation which would precede the exaltation through the resurrection, correspond with utterances found in either Matthew or Mark or both.[3] If one leaves out of account Lk. vi. 22 and xxii. 48 as being only relatively unique,[4] it is discovered that only one utterance is exclusively Lucan. That is the saying at the close of the story of Zacchaeus, 'For the Son of Man came to seek and to save that which was lost' (Lk. xix. 10).

[1] Cf. WMMC, pp. 249 ff.

[2] For the first group cf. Lk. ix. 26, xii. 8, 40, xvii. 24, 26, xxi. 27; for the second group Lk. xvii. 30, xviii. 8, xxi. 36.

[3] Cf. Lk. v. 24, vi. 5, vii. 34, ix. 22, 44, 58, xi. 30, xii. 10, xviii. 31 f., xxii. 22, xxiv. 7.

[4] Lk. vi. 22 pronounces blessing upon those who are hated and reproached and whose names are cast out as evil 'for the Son of Man's sake.' Mt. v. 11 speaks similarly of those who are persecuted 'for my sake.' In Lk. xxii. 48 Judas is asked, 'Betrayest thou the Son of Man with a kiss?'. This also has no parallel, but Luke xviii. 31, xxii. 22, and their synoptic parallels deal with the betrayal of the Son of Man.

The purpose of bringing salvation to the house of Zacchaeus, which is grounded in Jesus' broad declaration of the goal of His mission, confirms emphatically the view of the meaning of the title as intimating the heavenly, supernatural character of the Messiah. Jesus is not a mere man, but a heavenly Being who came to effect supernaturally the salvation of men. He was born indeed as a man, but even His human nature He owed to a supernatural act. And though He lived a life of privation and ignominy, did not have a place to lay His head, brought offence when He joined others in social intercourse, was mocked and insulted, betrayed by one of the twelve, and finally nailed to the cross, we are never allowed to lose sight of the fact that these human experiences were in the last analysis of startling incongruity because of His rightful claim of glory as the Son of Man. These experiences were endured therefore only as required by the divine plan of salvation and as a prelude to His own vindication and glory through the power of God. His essentially supernatural and glorious nature was to manifest itself through His resurrection, His session at God's right hand, and His coming on the clouds of heaven, but even in His earthly career He acted in the consciousness of His supreme dignity and power.

So supernatural indeed is Luke's pervasive presentation of Christ that the charge is sometimes levelled at him that, owing to his reverence for Jesus' person, he has been reluctant to leave traces of human emotions or expressions of stern and violent feeling.[1] Much is made, for example, of the fact that in reporting the stories of the healing of a leper and the feeding of the five thousand Luke is silent concerning the 'compassion' of Jesus where Mark makes mention of it (Mk. i. 41, vi. 34; Lk. v. 13, ix. 11 f.). Besides Luke does not include the story of the feeding of the four thousand where the third instance of mention of the compassion of Jesus is found (Mk. viii. 2). This charge rests, however, on a quite inadequate induction of the facts. If Luke omitted the reference to Jesus' compassion in these stories because such an emotion seemed to conflict with his views of the transcendence of Christ, why does he use the very term in motivating Jesus'

[1] Cf. Cadbury, *Style and Literary Method of Luke*, pp. 90 ff.; *Making*, p. 266; M. S. Enslin, *Christian Beginnings*, 1938, pp. 405 f. On a similar charge against Matthew, cf. WMMC, pp. 82 f., 219 f.

action in raising the widow's son at Nain (Lk. vii. 13)? Nor can one readily set aside as irrelevant two other instances of the word in Luke. Both the characterization of the good Samaritan in Lk. x. 33 and of the father of the prodigal son in Lk. xv. 20 as moved with compassion, though of course they do not describe Jesus' own emotional life, are evidently approved as actions by which men would demonstrate their divine sonship (cf. Lk. vi. 35) or even, in the second case, the nature of the divine love for the lost. How then can it be supposed that Luke regards compassion as incongruous with divine dignity! Moreover, it is a highly hazardous procedure to draw far-reaching conclusions from the silence of Luke as to certain details, especially since his narrative is marked by brevity of characterization.[1]

The mere fact, moreover, that Luke, in reporting the cleansing of the temple, omits any reference to His overturning of the tables and seats is taken as evidence of Luke's desire to suppress intimations that Jesus acted with violence.[2] Mark's narrative does in fact present vivid details of Jesus' wrathful and stirring action which are not found in Luke (Mk. xi. 15-18; cf. Lk. xix. 45 ff.). But it is far-fetched to conclude that Luke presents an essentially different picture of Jesus' emotional reactions. If Luke were concerned to avoid the impression that Jesus acted with violence and spoke with vehemence against the occupants of the temple, why should he include the pregnant statement that 'He began to cast out them that sold' and the unmild charge that they had made the house of prayer a den of robbers (Lk. xix. 45 f.)?[3]

The sternness of Jesus as portrayed by Mark is often contrasted with the gentleness of Jesus in Luke's Gospel, and this seems to find its chief support in the absence from Luke of various refer-

[1] Cadbury himself makes this observation. *Style and Literary Method*, pp. 79 ff., 127 f.

[2] Cf. Cadbury, *Style and Literary Method*, pp. 90 f.; Enslin, op. cit., p. 406.

[3] Luke is also sometimes said to have been influenced in his treatment of the story by his concern to soften the impression of hostility to Judaism. Luke does indeed show in the Gospel as well as in the Acts that Christians were not hostile to the worship of the temple as such. But the zeal of Jesus for the worship of God in the temple is revealed in its greatest intensity precisely through the strength of His emotional reaction to its abuse on the part of certain contemporaries. On the other hand, in the Gospel and Acts, no more than in the other Gospels, is there any evidence of a tendency to relieve the tension between Jesus and His disciples, on the one hand, and the representatives of current Judaism, on the other. Cf., e.g., Acts ii. 22 f., iii. 13.

ences to Jesus' anger, His rebuke of Peter and the like (cf. Mk. iii. 5, viii. 33).[1] Since in Mark also, as has been noticed, Jesus is motivated in His actions towards men by love and compassion, the sternness displayed there is by no means unrelieved. And so far as Luke is concerned, though certain expressions which might seem severe are missing, others are conspicuously present. For all of His gentleness and kindliness the Jesus of Luke is absolutely uncompromising in His demands. Although the rebuke of Peter is not mentioned, Luke alone tells of the rebuke of James and John when they requested that they be permitted to bid fire come down from heaven to consume the Samaritans who did not receive Jesus (Lk. ix. 51 ff.). Only the Jesus of Luke charges the disciples that, if a brother sin, they should rebuke him (Lk. xvii. 3). And in none of the Gospels is Jesus' demands for self-sacrifice as a condition of discipleship expressed as absolutely as in Luke:

> 'If any man cometh unto Me, and hateth not his own father, and mother, and wife, and children, and brethren, and sisters, yea, and his own life also, he cannot be My disciple' (Lk. xiv. 26).
>
> 'So therefore whosoever he be of you that renounceth not all that he hath, he cannot be My disciple' (Lk. xiv. 33).

It may be recalled that it was these sayings which Renan especially appealed to in support of his construction that Jesus, now no longer under the spell of the sunshine and green hills of Galilee, had ceased to be 'the delicate and joyous moralist of earlier days' but was rather 'the sombre giant whom a kind of sublime presentiment was casting more and more beyond the pale of humanity.'[2] Renan's construction is, to be sure, quite unscientific. The double image of Christ which he finds in the Gospels, amounting virtually to implications of schizophrenia, and the extremely arbitrary forcing of the data into a scheme of development, will satisfy the historian and the psychologist no more than the man of faith. Nevertheless, his reconstruction has served the useful purpose of concentrating attention upon features of the Gospel witness which all too commonly are overlooked or under-

[1] Cf. Cadbury, *Style and Literary Method*, p. 91; Enslin, op. cit., pp. 405 f.; Creed, op. cit., pp. lxii f.

[2] E. Renan, *Vie de Jésus*, 1863, p. 312.

estimated. In particular, Renan's characterization reminds us at this point that the Lucan portrait is by no means divested of the traits of firmness. Christ demands an exclusive devotion to Himself, one that requires the subordination of all other affections to one great overpowering affection for Himself. In this Gospel, then, the elements of firmness and gentleness, of severity and graciousness are blended together to create an overwhelming impression of One who was constantly controlled in His actions no less by the demands of righteousness than by those of love.

Another feature of the Lucan portrayal which ill agrees with the notion that this evangelist was concerned to depict Jesus as free from human infirmity is the place given to the prayers of Jesus. The other records likewise speak of Jesus' practice of prayer,[1] but Luke does so far more often. He not only described the prayer in the garden (Lk. xxii. 41 ff.) and on many other occasions such as the baptism and transfiguration (Lk. iii. 21, ix. 28 f.), but also indicates that Jesus' praying was habitual and prolonged (cf. Lk. v. 16, vi. 12, ix. 18, xi. 1). It is hardly an exaggeration therefore to state that, according to Luke, the entire ministry of Jesus was carried out in a spirit of dependence upon God. If Luke were deliberately recasting the gospel tradition with a view to the obliteration of features which might seem to represent Him as sharing human emotions and attitudes, we should be at a loss to understand the prominence given to Jesus' practice of prayer.

The Christ of Luke is not a new Christ. One who turns from the portraits of Matthew and Mark to contemplate that of Luke will immediately recognize the identity of the Person. Prolonged and painstaking attention to details will serve only to confirm the judgment gained from first impressions.

There are indeed notable differences in the testimony of the three evangelists. In Mark we discover a figure who, for all of the mystery that surrounds Him, stands out in rugged simplicity as the Son of God who unwaveringly marches to the cross to give His life as a ransom for many. The Matthaean portrait is more complex. The central motif of Mark is present, but in Matthew there is much besides. Jesus is disclosed as being a divine Person, and one also contemplates the lonely act of self-humiliation to

[1] Mk. i. 35, vi. 46, xiv. 32, 35, 39; Mt. xiv. 23, xxvi. 36, 39, 42, 44.

the death on the cross. But now the figure of Jesus appears in less severe isolation. A richer background is drawn and the future is more sharply delineated, and thus one comes to a fuller understanding of Christ's place in history. Matthew's witness is wonderfully suited for instruction and meditation. It lends itself to a contemplation which rests upon one feature and then another until the whole is seen in its wealth of detail.

Luke like Matthew contains the message of Mark. He appears to have left it largely undisturbed. And much of the distinctive contents of Matthew may be paralleled in Luke. But there are also extraordinary supplementary features in Luke, many of which have been dwelt upon in the foregoing chapters. Much of the colour of Luke is derived from the singular and fascinating contents of the birth narrative, the parables and other teaching in the middle chapters, and the account of the resurrection and the ascension of Christ.

In taking account of the supplementary character of Luke, however, one is far from doing full justice to the individuality of this Gospel. It is by no means to be gauged simply in terms of additions or omissions, for it has a unity and coherence of its own. The gospel was in a most important sense the common property of the Christian Church. No matter who proclaimed it, there was the necessity of faithfulness to what had been handed down. But it was proclaimed by different evangelists at different times and in different situations. In explaining the individuality of Luke, accordingly, one must consider various historical factors. These must have included Luke's own special aptitudes and qualifications as a writer, his opportunities for securing information, and his estimate of the needs of those for whom the finished work was intended. His unusual skill as a writer is evident from beginning to end. His personal contacts with Christians in centres like Jerusalem and Caesarea explain many of his unique contributions to our knowledge of Jesus' life and message. The choice of materials and manner of presentation were also influenced by his aim to provide such an exposition and defence of the origins of Christianity as would be most conducive to the establishment of the faith of persons like Theophilus. Theophilus was evidently a Gentile, and he must have been viewed as a representative of the Gentile world to which Luke, the Greek writer, could with peculiar insight and sympathy address the Gospel. His avoidance of Semitic forms and his silence on some points which would have been peculiarly obscure to persons uninstructed in Jewish beliefs and practices may be explained on this basis.

It remains most remarkable, however, that for all of the distinctiveness and individuality of Luke, it is impossible to single out perspectives that may be characterized as constituting *tendencies* of the Gospel. In the modern literature there have indeed been frequent allegations that Luke has edited the tradition and manipulated it in the interest of setting forth, consciously or unconsciously, his own special viewpoints. As the evidence has been examined, however, it has been found that it is impossible to set Luke sharply over against Matthew and Mark in regard to such matters as the lordship of Jesus and His atoning death or the coming of the kingdom of God.

Though there are unique features and special interests and emphases, there is nothing to disturb the unity of the testimony. The beauty and charm of the whole seem to be due to a skilful blending of a wealth of detail into an inspiring single impression. Luke did not believe that religious devotion flourished in the absence of earnest meditation upon historical truth, and we should therefore prove untrue to his approach to his subject if the suggestion were made that one might be indifferent to the details of Luke and yet gain a true appreciation of it. Our impression is rather that, though the details grip our attention, none is so conspicuous that we can long contemplate it without observing that it blends into the total representation. Luke's witness to Christ is therefore a superb work of devotion and adoration. And it is most appropriate that the first and last scenes of the Gospel find their setting in the temple at Jerusalem.

INDEXES

I. NAMES AND SUBJECTS

II. SCRIPTURE REFERENCES

JOHN

ACTS

H. Sp.

Dr Hoyler of 1st Bap. Fresno. on H Sp warned against speaking of H Sp as "influence" like ^power^ electricity surging thru wire. He said: When we get the H. Sp. we get all of him. Can't have 1/2 of a "person". H Sp = a person

I disagree: He's a Presence, Person limits him to human shape, ~~He~~ I can receive a part of my ^wife^ wife even if she is a person

103 Jesus repeated himself " " " doublets

110 new age has indeed come; Jesus was resurrected.

111-112 on the spec. Lk. material -- "Journey"

120-f on Lk 23:8-12 on Herod "that fox"

Ch8 The "Kingdom" in Lk. (K. Tile)

127 on Theophilus

156 Lk 9:27 as meaning the Church.

152f Christology, 165f on Lord 169-170

next ingathering, be sure to include Linda Sandeep.

Urg

I'd like the salary schedules cut - so that only that concerns the individual gets distributed from here on.

W: Send your note to the officer re: the Pres. off. training this weekend.

Dick Holt needs to bring in nom. report Sunday.

I forgot to get the $940 Brazil dues before admin.

Dave: Have you got to the new members of the Dec. class yet?; W: phone their Deacons to see if they have? Then Bill Nash - on steward call on Drs.

Jim Williams
Sharon